OUTLAWS
and
LAWMEN
of the
WEST

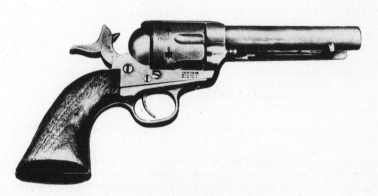

M.A. Macpherson
Eli MacLaren

LONE
PINE

The Publisher: Lone Pine Publishing

2311 - 96 Street
Edmonton, AB T6N 1G3
Canada

1808 B Street NW, Suite 140
Auburn, WA 98001
USA

Website: www.lonepinepublishing.com

Canadian Cataloguing in Publication Data
Macpherson, M.A. (Margaret A.), 1959–
    Oulaws and lawmen of the West
    Includes bibliographical references.
    ISBN 1-55105-164-8

    1. Outlaws—West (U.S.)—Biography. 2. Outlaws—West (U.S.)—Fiction. I. MacLaren, E. (Eli) II. Title.
HV6785.M32 2000   364.1'092'278   C00-910241-8

Editorial Director: Nancy Foulds
Project Editor: Eli MacLaren
Production Manager: Jody Reekie
Book Design: Heather Markham
Cover Design: Rob Weidemann-
Layout & Production: Arlana Anderson-Hale
Maps: Ian Sheldon

The authors gratefully acknowledge the contribution of Daniel Asfar, who wrote the story on Sam Bass.

Cover Photographs: Three Cattle Rustlers, photo by Bennett and Burrell, courtesy of the Museum of New Mexico, Neg. No. 14264; Billy the Kid's Colt .44, courtesy of the University of Oklahoma Library Western History Collections; Robert Ford, courtesy of the Pony Express Historical Association; The Wild Bunch, courtesy of the Wyoming State Archives.

Photographs Courtesy of: Montana Historical Society (p. 14, 956-061; p. 30-31, 940-703; p. 37, 942-073); California Historical Society, Luke Fay College (p. 44, FN-00947); University of Oklahoma Library, Western History Collection (p. 64, 2135; p. 80, 2136; p. 130-131, 2278; p. 138, 2108; p. 168, 2155); Pony Express Historical Association (p. 82, p. 105, p. 106-107, p. 108); Lincoln County Heritage Trust (p. 110); Museum of New Mexico (pp. 116-117, photo by J.R. Riddle, Courtesy of Museum of New Mexico, Neg. No. 76100); Kansas State Historical Society (p. 150); Vancouver Public Library, Special Collections (p. 188, VPL 9951B); Buffalo Bill Historical Center, Cody, Wyoming (p. 200); Wyoming State Archives (p. 202-203, 1591); Utah State Historical Archives (p. 224, 12932, used by permission, all rights reserved).

We acknowledge the financial support of the Government of Canada through the Canada Book Fund (CBF) for our publishing activities.

PC: P5

CONTENTS

FOREWORD

If a mean, gritty, unshaven, tobacco-chewing, lasso-whirling gunman were to stomp up to you wearing leather riding boots and a sombrero in the middle of a dusty street and growl a single command—"Draw!"—you would immediately know what he was talking about, and it would have nothing to do with pencil crayons or paper. Through early newspaper accounts, dime novels, books, cartoons and movies, the Wild West has become about as familiar to us today as our own modern world. In fact, it is so firmly planted in our imagination that most of us are no longer sure how it got there.

But the Wild West does have a traceable history. It emerged as the result of specific causes, lasted for a certain period of time—and then seeped away again after having left its indelible mark.

In 1803, the United States doubled its size in one fell swoop. On April 30 of that year, President Thomas Jefferson made the Louisiana Purchase, a payment of $15 million in exchange for an enormous piece of land stretching from New Orleans to southern Montana. Everything between the Mississippi River and the Rocky Mountains suddenly became part of the United States. Eastern law began to creep across the Mississippi and push back the frontier when

Louisiana, Arkansas, Missouri and Iowa were admitted as States to the Union, but politicians, lawyers and sheriffs could not hope to overtake the first waves of ambitious farmers and adventurers.

Of course, the frontier was not the edge of nothing. Beyond it was the rich diversity of the Indian nations, who had used the land for centuries. Although the United States eagerly supported expansion, it increasingly recognized that the settlers were introducing incorrigible problems to the ancient Indian cultures, and segregation was attempted. Beginning in 1820, entire nations, including the Cherokee, Seminole and Chickasaw Indians, were forced from their homes in the East and relocated in the land west of Missouri. In 1834, the Indian Intercourse Act drew a clear line up the western edge of Arkansas, Missouri and Iowa by creating the Indian Territory to the west of these states. The Act did much to cement a frontier. Missouri was regarded as a border state right up until the end of the 19th century; in the 1860s, friends of Henry Plummer thought of St. Louis as the jumping-off point into the great untamed lands of the West, and the notorious Dalton brothers were still exploiting the lawlessness of the Indian Territory as late as the 1890s.

The wave of settlement had long since swept on. In 1821, Stephen F. Austin led a brave party of settlers into what would become Texas. The Mexican government was initially grateful for people who would till the land and drive off the hostile Indians, but as the 1830s wore on, it grew anxious over the number of slave-owning Americans that were setting up successful cotton plantations on Mexican land. A crackdown began, but in 1835 the Texas Rebellion broke out. After a terrible defeat at the Alamo, the Texans under the leadership of Samuel Houston struck back and routed their Mexican enemies in the battle at San Jacinto on April 21, 1836.

Texas then applied for admission to the United States, but was refused. Powerful abolitionists did not want to see another slave state join the Union and upset the already precarious balance; the United States was dangerously divided on the issue of slavery. Only after Southerners lobbied for nine long years was Texas formally annexed by the United States, in 1845.

The annexation sparked the Mexican War. The tensions building over the issue of slavery were put aside between 1846 and 1848, when Americans united for the cause of expansion. Many believed that it was the "manifest destiny" of the United States to become a great nation stretching from the Atlantic to the Pacific Ocean. The U.S. Army made this dream come true. The Mexicans were beaten, and, in the Treaty of Guadalupe Hidalgo, were forced to cede much of their land to the victors. Once again, the United States dramatically increased in size. New Mexico, Arizona, Utah, Nevada, California, and parts of Colorado and Wyoming all came under American jurisdiction as a result of the Mexican War.

At the end of the Mexican War, a remarkable discovery was made. In 1848, near Sacramento, a man named James W. Marshall was helping build a sawmill for the California landowner John Sutter when something shiny in the streambed caught his eye. It was gold. His discovery touched off the single most impressive migration in American history. What had before been a slow trickle became a crashing tide as Easterners rushed west in 1849 to stake a claim. Towns sprang up wherever the trace of a glitter was found. As the years wore on, the gold rush spread. By 1860, Montana was in its grip;

Western Canada, Alaska and the Colorado of Butch Cassidy would also be deluged by gold-hungry adventurers.

The gold rush was an inextricable element of what we know as the Wild West. Many people were caught up in its current, not the least of whom were Black Bart, Henry Plummer, Tiburcio Vasquez and the father of Frank and Jesse James. For some, the time was one of incredible riches, but for many the gold rush brought only disillusionment, destruction and death. Striking gold was one thing; efficiently mining it and safely transporting it back to civilization was quite another. A whole generation of highwaymen, cutthroats and thieves was born from the lawlessness and frenzy that took over when innumerable fortune seekers poured into the wilderness in search of gold. Only those who could defend themselves could hold onto the slippery wealth.

Meanwhile, a lesser stream of settlers was moving west from Illinois. In 1847, the first Mormons led by Brigham Young reached Great Salt Lake in modern-day Utah. There they founded Salt Lake City. The Mormons were industrious farmers and did much to create good and secure communities in an otherwise difficult, if not hostile, wilderness. By 1870, Salt Lake City was a major commercial center located on the first American transcontinental railroad.

With the first thrill of the gold rush over, national attention returned to the explosive issue of slavery. The chief cause of the Civil War was the following issue: should slavery be permitted in the new territories of the West, or not? The Missouri Compromise of 1820 had tried to settle the matter by admitting Missouri to the Union as a slave state and drawing a line across the West just above the 36th parallel. Territories south of the line would be slave and those north of it would be free. An uneasy compromise between North and South ensued, but in 1854, Indian Territory was vastly reduced in size by the creation of Kansas and Nebraska. Missourians in particular now assumed that, in order to keep the balance, the government would designate Kansas a slave state and Nebraska free. The anti-slavery side did not see the matter the same way, and when they began aggressively to settle Kansas, fighting broke out along the Kansas-Missouri border. "Bleeding Kansas" was the nickname of the state during this period of raids.

When the Republican Abraham Lincoln was elected in 1861, South Carolina declared its independence from the United States—and the Civil War began. Eleven Southern states allied themselves against the North and formed the Confederacy under President Jefferson Davis. Bloodshed swept through the countryside, but as the war progressed the industrial superiority of the North gradually made itself felt. The military campaigns lasted until 1865—when Confederate General Robert E. Lee surrendered to Union General Ulysses S. Grant at Appomattox—but the violence continued well into the postwar period of Reconstruction.

The Civil War was the greatest catalyst for the Wild West. The destruction it wrought and the heritage of violence it introduced desensitized a whole generation to bloodletting and carnage. It transformed the pistol from a dangerous tool into an essential means of self-preservation. While abolishing slavery, it also ruined the economy of the South and ushered in a crushing poverty from which many felt they could escape only by breaking the law. The Civil War was a time of enormous upheaval and its participants should perhaps be judged sympathetically, but it cannot be denied that the war sanctioned violence on a massive scale and impressed countless minds with its free-wheeling and destructive spirit.

Thus, in a relatively short period of time, more than half a continent was added to the young country called the United States and infused with a spirit of hardy if not violent self-preservation. The new space seemed boundless, and during the years when traditional law sought to establish itself, the settlers were clearly faced with the prospect of wringing out an existence from the rugged environment with only the power of their own two hands to help them. This freedom—both exhilarating and terrifying—is what we now think of as "wild."

The Wild West was a world of young law, chaotic uncertainty and wide-open freedom, in which strong individuality soared above all other values. And of those early individualists, though many more stories are yet to be told, the ones that caused the greatest stir, the ones that have leapt from the hard dirt of fact to the glossy pages of fiction, were the mean, gritty, gun-toting types: the outlaws.

Jack Slade was a brutish but sometimes soft-hearted man prone to drunken rampages in which he killed remorselessly, but he was nevertheless hired to enforce the law in Colorado in the 1850s. By 1864, in what is now Montana, the community was tired of his violence and strung him up vigilante-style. Dead before his beautiful widow could say good-bye, Jack lingered in a tin-lined coffin filled with alcohol until she could cart him away for burial.

At about the same time in nearby Bannack, the cold-eyed Henry Plummer landed a job as sheriff. Mystery shrouds the facts of his death. Was he really the ringleader of a terrible gang of killers and robbers—the so-called Gang of Innocents—who went to their death denying their guilt? Or was he merely an innocent man caught up in forces beyond his control?

John Wesley Hardin, the fastest draw in Reconstruction Texas, murdered his way through the period following the Civil War. An outlaw in trouble for years, Hardin's killing spree finally ended on a train filled with Texas Rangers when his gun tangled with his suspenders and he netted a 25-year jail sentence. A year after his release, in 1895, he was shot dead.

Our outlaw lineup would not be complete without Jesse James, the action-hungry, murderous bandit who terrorized banks and railroads and who fascinated newspapermen, songwriters and loyal followers forever after. Jesse and his older brother Frank emerged from the Civil War bent on revenge; their first bank heist, early in 1866, netted $60,000 of Union money. Based mainly in Missouri, they became the most notorious outlaws of their time, robbing widely through the West in the 1870s with mercilessness and bravado that became legendary. But Jesse was also a family man, and died in 1882 at home, a bullet through the back of the head.

In the 1870s as well, Sam Bass, gambler, con man, ex-farmer, ex-logger and ex-cowboy, rode into Denton, Texas, and began a short-lived career as teamster to lawman "Dad" Eagan before being lured into a life of crime. His chief claim to fame was a train robbery at Big Springs, Nebraska, and he and his gang roamed far and wide in the West trying to re-create that glory. Sam died young after the "The Bass War," which pitted five hoodlums against 200 lawmen. Sam had a kind streak, and it was that characteristic that gained him fame in "The Ballad of Sam Bass."

Off to the west in Arizona, in 1877, Billy the Kid killed his first man. Not yet 20 years old, Billy soon amassed a reputation as a hooligan, rustler, horseman and crack marksman. Billy's participation in the Lincoln County War, and his miraculous escapes from justice, earned him legendary status. But the law caught up with Billy before too long.

Back farther east in the late 1880s and early 1890s, the audacious Dalton Gang achieved infamy and became legends of the West. Their start came when older brother Frank was viciously murdered; most of the remaining brothers joined to form a gang of nighttime marauders, striking railroads and banks throughout Kansas and Oklahoma. Their careers peaked in October 1892 when they simultaneously hit two banks in Coffeyville, Kansas. The result was one of the most spectacular and well-documented shoot-outs of the West.

Butch Cassidy is among the best-known outlaws of the West. Born in Utah, Butch began his career as a train robber in 1887, and he was still in the business over 20 years later. Along the way, his Wild Bunch grew to include an Easterner—later nicknamed the Sundance Kid—and Butch and Sundance formed an unbeatable team that ended only with death. Since then, their fame has only grown.

Pinkerton detectives, state Rangers and other lawmen, plus the increasing march of population, automobiles, telephones, fingerprinting and street lights across the West, gradually put an end to the free-wheeling outlaw days known to these men.

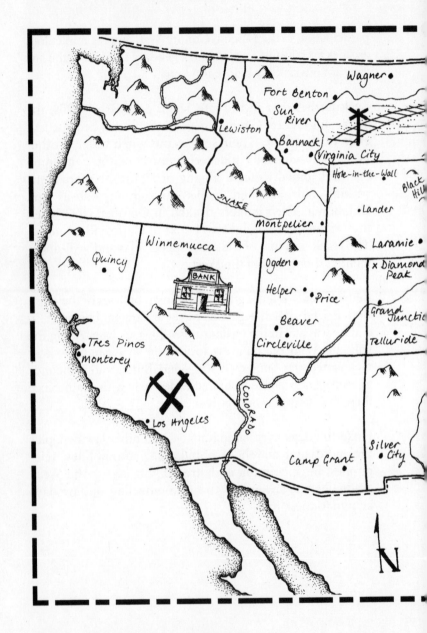

THE WEST OF THE OUTLAWS AND LAWMEN

VIRGINIA CITY, MONTANA, 1866

1

Jack Slade

It was his reputation for toughness and his devil-may-care attitude that bought Slade his first real job.

Why couldn't you have shot him like a man? Instead you've strung him up like an animal."

These were the anguished words of Jack Slade's widow when she rode her lathered horse into Virginia City, Montana, in 1864, and found that a vigilante committee had already hanged her beloved husband.

Joseph Alfred Slade, better known to his friends and enemies as Jack, thought nothing of shooting a man, and when he was drunk, he would put a bullet in a man's back rather than buy him a glass of whiskey.

One of the most feared men in the West, Slade was as unpredictable as a spring tornado. He ran from sweet to sour as quickly as most men could open a bottle of homebrew. The sober Jack Slade won the friendship of Mark Twain, despite what the latter called his "awful history." On a drinking binge, however, Slade was a wild gunfighter who murdered anyone who stood in his way, regardless of literary eminence.

Virginia Slade, his wife, who had her own daunting reputation for wild behavior as well as beauty, cut her man down from the makeshift gallows on that mid-March morning in 1864 and ordered a coffin be built and lined with tin. There, in raw alcohol, the fuel that drove the murderous rampages of Jack Slade, the man with the split and dangerous personality floated for months while Virginia grieved.

Jack was born in 1824 in Carlyle, Illinois. He received little public education and by the time he was a teenager, he was hungry for adventure. An exciting possibility of exploit presented itself in the outbreak of the Mexican War in 1840s, and the young Slade signed up with Company A of the First Regiment of Illinois Foot Volunteers. The army gave him a chance to check out the vast country of the American Southwest. It also gave him a taste for booze, the liquid fire that would eventually become his undoing.

He returned to Carlyle in 1848 but a drunken argument with a local man resulted in a brawl that left the man dead. Jack Slade had crushed his opponent's head with a boulder grabbed from the ditch. He had killed his first fellow citizen, which prompted him to leave Illinois for good, fearing for his neck. He would try his fortunes west of the Mississippi.

It was his reputation for toughness and his devil-may-care attitude that bought Slade his first real job. One day in 1855 he and a friend were riding the stagecoach line, the Overland, between two stations in Colorado, when they were attacked by three Sioux warriors. Slade shot all three Natives down before his friend could even draw his revolver. When the story was told at the trailhead, Ben Ficklin, owner of the Overland Line, got wind of it and was immediately interested in Jack.

He was looking for a man to take over Julesburg, a major stopover point along the 300-mile-long Sweetwater Division of the Overland Line. Located near the South Platte River near Fort Sedgwick, Julesburg, with a population of about 2000, was considered the starting-off point for the Bozeman trail. It was also considered a crazy, murderous town where at least one man was shot every day. Killing was rampant. It was one of the Line's toughest postings and one in dire need of reform.

Julesburg was named after Jules Reni (in some accounts spelled Bene), the man whom Ben Ficklin was looking to replace. Ficklin had long been suspicious, and was now convinced that Reni was misusing company money. Bales of hay, kept for the stagecoach horses, were continually catching fire. Ficklin suspected that they were being purposely torched in order that Reni's friends might have the privilege of selling the company new ones. Some of the company money, of course, would always find its way back to Reni's pocket.

Horses were also being stolen. Reni was always after Ficklin to give out rewards for stolen ponies. His friends reaped the profits and, as Ficklin suspected, Reni was taking a cut. The long and the short of it was that the Overland was being cheated by one of its own superintendents. Ficklin's aim was to replace Jules Reni with a new, tough recruit.

When Slade came along, he was no friend to Jules Reni. Their first confrontation was the beginning of a personal feud that would not end until one of them was dead.

Slade walked into Reni's office in Julesburg and silently passed him his walking papers. "Seems like I'm your replacement," said the stocky Slade, after Reni had looked at the papers.

"You won't last a week," was Reni's reply.

"I'm going to last, but you've already overstayed your welcome. I'll give you a couple of hours to collect up your stuff and git the hell out of this town."

Reni's eyes narrowed menacingly. "You and who else?" he challenged.

Slade pulled out his revolver and placed its barrel against Reni's temple. "Any other questions?" he asked.

Jules Reni knew when he had been beaten but he wasn't about to leave his domain like a whipped dog, tail between his legs. His final words were chilling: "I'll see you buried, Slade." The self-appointed king of Julesburg had been dethroned, but both men knew that they hadn't seen the last of each other.

Slade was determined to bring law and order to the Sweetwater Division of the Overland line. He started by overhauling his office and posting his name on a placard—J.A. Slade, Superintendent—so everyone could see that a new era had started. He knew that a name without a reputation behind it was worthless, so as soon as an opportunity arose, Slade went out to prove he meant business.

A little while later, two men rode into Julesburg with word that a stagecoach had been held up just two miles out of town. Slade gathered a posse and hurried out after the bandits, who thought that Jules Reni was still in charge of the Overland outfit. They were in for a nasty surprise.

When Slade and his men caught up to the four outlaws, they wasted no time. The robbers were tried, judged guilty and sentenced to hang within half an hour of the confrontation. Four bodies dangled from a rancher's gatepost by the time Slade and his men started back to town. The hanged men spoke loudly for Slade's new crusade of cleaning up the Sweetwater line. Their bodies, left for two days, indicated to everyone who saw them not to mess with Overland. They declared louder than any words possibly could that there was a new superintendent in charge and that he was no pushover.

For the next few months, Slade rode up and down the line checking stations at 25-mile intervals. He insisted that farmers selling hay for horses sell pure feed, not feed mixed with weeds and branches. To drive home his point, he chained a crooked farmer to a log, had his men build a huge bonfire, and threatened to throw him into the roaring blaze. The hysterical farmer swore to change his ways, and before long, Slade's unorthodox means of getting people to comply with his tough standards brought business practices to a higher level. The Sweetwater Division was being reformed by a known criminal, and he was doing a fine job.

Slade found the woman of his dreams in local Julesburg beauty Virginia Dale. With a reputation for riding and shooting that equaled his own, Virginia was a good match for the wild Jack. He made no attempts to tame her and the two lived an extremely volatile life together.

In the spring of 1858, Slade had a run-in with his nemesis Jules Reni. It almost cost him his life. About 25 miles up the line, west of Julesburg, Slade came across Reni at a camp. He wasn't expecting trouble and by all accounts was unarmed. Reni saw him standing in range and rapidly emptied the contents of his Colt .45 into Slade's body. Either Reni was an awfully bad shot, or Slade's skin was tougher than shoe leather, for Slade somehow managed to stay erect despite being hit each time.

Slade staggered forward, while the terrified Reni, amazed that his enemy refused to fall, stepped back to retrieve a double-barreled shotgun. He raised the rifle to his shoulder and let loose a last shot to the bullet-ridden body of Jack Slade. When the buckshot hit him in a hundred spots, he fell at last, and Reni turned tail and ran. He should have put one last bullet into the head of the fallen man for good measure if he'd wanted to be sure Slade was well and truly dead, but he must have figured no man could live with that much lead in his body. Slade proved Reni wrong.

Slade's men gathered around to look at the bleeding body of their fallen leader. They were shocked to hear Slade mutter, "God-damn Reni. God-damn coward." The tough-as-nails outlaw refused to die. On the operating table, while an army surgeon plucked the bullets from his hide, Slade could think of nothing but revenge.

It seemed that Jules Reni was cut from the same cloth as Jack Slade. Both men cheated death when all odds said they would die.

After shooting Slade, Reni was hunted down and hanged by Overland men. He was strung up by the neck and hoisted in three yanks to a high tree limb. Somehow he survived, despite turning an alarming shade of purple, and was brought back down to earth with his neck intact. He swore he'd leave the area but he did not do so quickly enough. Jack Slade and Jules Reni had one more vicious confrontation before them, and it was this third encounter that saw luck run out for one of them.

Nursed by his wife Virginia, Slade recovered from his wounds. After having mended, he was given a new posting by his boss. The Rocky Ridge division of the Overland line, a couple of hundred miles west, had attracted the criminal element once the Sweetwater division had been cleaned up. Slade had new territory and his new mandate was to get Jules Reni and let every one in Rocky Ridge know about it.

The opportunity to exact revenge came sooner than Slade thought. In 1859, Reni was captured by a few of Slade's men and brought back to his property. There he died an agonizing and inhumane death.

Slade had been drinking whiskey on the morning Reni was dragged in, bound and defiant. The Overland superintendent decided to make a spectacle of him. He had him lashed to a snubbing pole out in the yard, took a long swallow of whiskey, and then pulled his gun and shot off two fingers from Reni's right hand. As Reni screamed in agony, Slade went back inside his house to have another snort. He stepped back into the doorway a half hour later and calmly shot off Reni's kneecaps. Another drink, another part was blown of Reni's body. It was an agonizing way to die and Slade, who at the end of the day had consumed two quarts of whiskey, seemed to enjoy it. During the last hour of Reni's life, Slade reportedly roared with laugher.

The body was a bloody pulp by the time Reni was dead, and Jack Slade a drunken and slurring braggart. In front of a number of horrified witnesses, he went up to the body of his enemy, drew a huge hunting knife and sliced off Reni's ears. It was the final straw for the people of the community.

Yes, Reni was a bad apple. Yes, they knew of the previous attack against Slade. Yes, the personal feud was well known among the citizenry, but surely no person should have to die the way Reni did, publicly dismembered while Jack Slade drank and laughed. Slade was supposed to represent the law, but his methods had gotten out of hand. The punishment had, in fact, proven worse than the initial crime. Slade was a man who inspired sheer terror when he was drinking. And Jack Slade had started to drink a lot.

His personality switched from good to bad during drinking binges. It wasn't uncommon for Slade to ride his horse into a saloon and start shooting at anyone who looked at him the wrong way. It was often said that he could shoot the buttons off a man's coat. What wasn't mentioned was the angle at which he did so.

Needing only to pull out the subtle, gruesome threat of Jules Reni's wizened ears to get a free drink, Slade drank hard and long, and when something he perceived as unjust happened, he was the first to shout out righteous indignation. He was also the first to try and right any wrongs that fell upon innocent victims.

In the summer of 1861 Slade got word that two men, Charley Bacon and Harry Smith, had killed a Dr. Bartholomew over a dispute about wages near Independence Rock, Wyoming. The physician was survived by his wife and two young children. Slade wired ahead to Joe Plante, owner of the general store. He told him, "Get two ropes ready, I'll be into town soon."

The two bandits were drinking and playing cards with an older man when Jack Slade rode up to the doctor's ranch. Slade did not take time to introduce himself. Bacon went for his gun, and Slade sent a bullet straight into his shoulder as a reminder of good behavior. All three men were hanged, even the old man in the card game, allegedly for "keeping such bad company." Before they were lynched, Slade had them empty their pockets. He took the money and presented it to the widow Bartholomew.

"Something to keep the children with," he explained, plunking down $523. He didn't say that some of the money had come from the pockets of an innocent man who just happened to be in the wrong place at the wrong time and now dangled from a roof beam. The widow expressed a desire to go back east to her home in Omaha, and Slade went to the trouble of selling her ranch for her and giving her the proceeds. His acts of kindness were totally incongruous with his acts of unmitigated, vengeful rage.

The Overland Stage Company had started to worry about Slade's activities. The drinking sprees were becoming more voracious and Slade's behavior more unpredictable. When he went into any of the numerous saloons on the 500-mile-long Rocky Ridge and Sweetwater divisions, people gave him a wide berth. Depending on his mood, Slade would either buy a fellow a bottle or crack it over his head. He developed a mania for shooting the tops off bottles and shattering shot glasses.

Slade in a bar meant flying bullets. Mirrors, bars, counters and even walls of various saloons smashed to the ground when Jack Slade was on the rampage. He was a man out of control, intent on destruction. His degenerating behavior caused Ben Ficklin, owner of the Overland line, to re-think his decision to have Slade in charge. While he had imposed peace on the line, he was still at war within himself, and his battle with the bottle was getting him into more and more trouble.

The incident that forced Ficklin to give Slade his walking papers was a mid-summer occurrence in 1862. A plastered Slade rode his horse straight into a nondescript store in Fort Halleck to get some tobacco. The horse, unaccustomed to being in such a confined space, reared, and Slade hit his head on the ceiling. Three soldiers and the shopkeeper laughed. They were not laughing 10 minutes later, when Slade had wrecked the store's interior and thrown each of the men and all of the merchandise out into the street.

Unfortunately for him, the store that Slade had trashed was a goods supply store of the United States Army, and the Army was the biggest customer of the Overland line. Ficklin got the word from his superior: Get rid of that superintendent. With employees like that, the Sweetwater and Rocky Ridge divisions didn't need thieves. Ficklin didn't want to risk business and, besides, Jack Slade's drinking and smashing sprees had become a major liability. In August 1862, after serving the company for two and a half years, Jack Slade was fired from the Overland line.

In the fall of 1862, Virginia convinced her husband to leave Colorado and move to southwestern Montana, where a gold rush was in full swing. Some time in 1863, they bought a plot of land two miles outside of Virginia City, which had just sprung up as a result of gold being found at Alder Gulch. Under the not-so-gentle persuasion of his wife, Slade endeavored to stay away from the bottle.

But Jack Slade had too much energy in him to live quietly within the bounds of the law. He needed excitement and if a community didn't provide it, he'd make it himself.

In March 1864 Slade went on his last drinking binge. He went from saloon to saloon in Virginia City, matching drink for drink with anyone who cared to compete with him, hollering, breaking things, shooting at lamp posts and mocking anybody who fell by the wayside, too drunk to continue the brawling orgy.

Slade's timing was off, way off.

During his period of relative sobriety the tenor of the times had changed. A few months before his last rampage, a Virginia City vigilance committee had been formed and between the end of December 1863 and February 1864 the group had hanged quite a few suspected criminals. It was clean-up time in Montana and the vigilantes were out for blood. Slade was a man living on borrowed time and his actions were not deemed acceptable.

Slade's penultimate affront to justice was neither brutally violent nor wantonly destructive. On the evening of March 8, after an eight-day spree of riotous howling, shooting and drinking in wild abandon, Slade and some of his cronies went to a traveling theater performance and disrupted the show by firing their guns and yelling obscenities at the actors. Virginia City's elite were in attendance, including Jim Williams, a member of the vigilance committee. He was disgusted by Slade's unruly behavior and decided it would not continue.

Very early the next morning, a drunk and staggering Slade met up with a milk delivery man doing his rounds at dawn. Slade asked him for a drink of milk, and, afraid to slight the drunken, slurring outlaw, the milkman passed over a gallon of fresh milk. Slade swallowed his fill, but some slopped on his shirt, at which point he dumped the remainder of the gallon over the head of the timid milkman.

It was a minor incident compared to the killing and torturing that preceded it, but it was just enough to tip the scales against Slade. The sheriff of Virginia City was contacted and a warrant for Slade's arrest was issued by Alexander Davis, acting judge of the community. The charge was one of disturbing the peace.

Still drunk and raging, Slade immediately ripped up the warrant when it was handed to him. He happened upon Judge Davis at Pfouts's and Russell's store, drew his revolver and lay it against the temple of the startled judge.

"You're my bail," whispered Slade into Davis's ear. "Anything happens to me, happens to you, too. Understand?" And with that, he stormed away, elbowing people roughly out of his way. Slade headed straight for a saloon and proceeded to down a good half-bottle of whiskey. He was not about to be brought in by any lily-livered, honey-talking theater aficionados who wouldn't know a pearl-handled revolver from a pig's snout.

It was not until the next morning, March 10, 1864, that the vigilance committee took action against Slade. Jim Williams had rounded up almost 200 men in the area, thinking that he'd have to take the wild, shooting devil-of-a-man by force. Miners, shop keepers and ranchers were all part of the posse that was going to subdue the renegade Overland lawman. Slade's gig was up, and the threat of the noose loomed. The vigilance committee, led by Williams, had already met in secret and decided that Slade had to be hanged. He was a bad example and a menace to the good citizens of Virginia City. Some felt it a shame, but the majority agreed that the deed had to be done if peace and good behavior were to prevail.

Slade had sobered up some by this time and, in typical fashion, was making his rounds to apologize to people whose property he had destroyed in his drunken rampage. He was at P.F. Pfouts's store when the vigilantes came calling.

Jim Williams stepped forward from the group and called Slade's name. "We want you," he said.

As Slade left the store he came face to face with 200 men who wanted his hide. He knew the time had come for him to face what he had made so many others face before him. There would be no trial, no call of innocence or guilt. The noose was made and the place ready.

From a crossbeam of a corral gate in a place called Daylight Gulch, Joseph Alfred Slade, a man who could be both very, very good, and very, very bad, was hanged by the neck.

By the time his wife arrived, he was dead. Spitting venom, she swore the city that bore her name would never have the body of her husband laid in its merciless grounds. Instead, she ordered the special coffin with the tin lining and, as befit her late husband, had it filled to the brim with alcohol.

Sluicing about in the stuff that had fueled his raging bravado, Jack Slade was hauled back to his homestead by his beautiful and heartbroken Virginia.

A few days later, she had Jack loaded onto a wagon and proceeded to take his body south across the mountains to Salt Lake City. He was buried in July in a Mormon cemetery. Saturated with liquor, the man who walked the thin line between order and chaos was finally laid to rest.

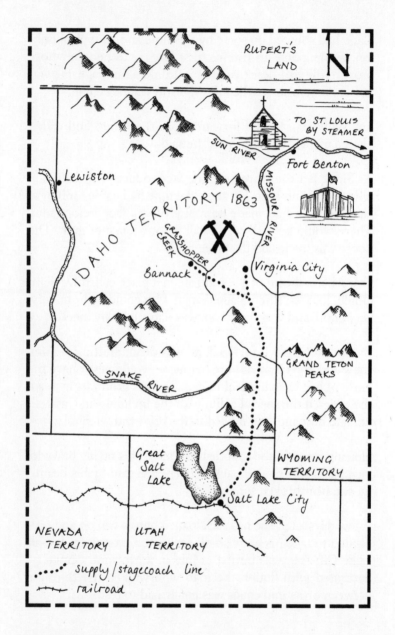

IDAHO TERRITORY

2

Henry Plummer and the Vigilantes

Was he a desperado, a fugitive from the law?
Beneath his patient, judicious calm lurked a surging
power, and Jack Cleveland had gone and provoked it.

For many years, history branded Henry Plummer an evil killer. He was long thought to be the organizer of the notorioius Gang of Innocents, a group of men who allegedly terrorized the Montana gold fields in the early 1860s. But recent work has thrown that reputation into question. Was Henry Plummer a villain, a kingpin of crime? Or was he a man of justice on whom Lady Luck did not smile? The people who could answer these questions would gladly have done so—had they been given the chance.

James and Granville Stuart, the first to discover gold in what is now western Montana, took an instant liking to Henry Plummer when they met him and his companion Charles Reeves on the trail one day. Though he beat them handily in a friendly poker game, they invited him up to Gold Creek with them, which they themselves had recently named.

Plummer declined. He was through with the frantic stampede for gold and planned to go back east, to his roots. From Fort Benton, he would hire a boat and take the 3000-mile-long trip down the Missouri River to St. Louis. Whether he thought that the Civil War—the conflict on the other side of the continent was then at its height— was a better background for his courage, or simply remembered fondly the place where law was an established institution and not the exhausting responsibility of lonely individuals, he did not say. He bid farewell to Reeves, and headed northeast. The Stuart brothers were sorry to see him go.

James and Granville Stuart were the first to sift the sparkling treasure from mountain streams east of the Continental Divide, but they were soon joined by hundreds of others. By September 1862, when Plummer and the Stuarts had their poker game, the gold rush had reached Grasshopper Creek and the foundation for the little mining town of Bannack was laid. At first it was no more than a camp of tents in an alpine valley, but as the gold fever spread, saloons, bakeries, butcher shops and outfitters' stations sprang up on the grassy banks along the creek, and the temporary shelters became homes. The main supply line came up from Salt Lake City, over 300 miles to the south. A couple of logs served as a rudimentary bridge between the two halves of the town. The miners' chief interest lay in working the streams, and finding a way to keep straight the question of which claim belonged to whom.

BANNACK IN THE 1860S

The community of Bannack invented justice all over again. During its first winter, its population of 500 was mostly men. These men would not receive an officially appointed magistrate from President Lincoln until the following spring, and even then, not many of the miners could have named the jurisdiction into which they fell. They were simply a bunch of men who found themselves thrown into one another's company by a common economic interest. And each day, the economy became more interesting: when winter set in, over $700,000 in gold had been sluiced from the streams.

The miners concocted a judicial alternative to the chaos that reigned in mountain country. They set up a little court. The miners' court was only as good as the men appointed to its offices, but it did successfully regulate the way newcomers could lay claim to a stretch of river. It also provided a mechanism for the settling of disputes, should they arise. And since it was fully the product of the those who lived in Bannack, Bannack fully agreed to abide by its rules.

Charlie Reeves was surprised to see his old aquaintance Henry Plummer in Bannack on November 23, 1862. When Reeves asked him what he was up to, Plummer laughed and confessed that he had not made it east. He had hired on at the government-run Sun River Farm 60 miles west of Fort Benton, where the missionary James Vail was living with his wife, two children, and sister-in-law. Vail feared an attack by the Blackfeet whom he had come to serve, and so hired Plummer and a man named Jack Cleveland to help defend the mission. Plummer had fallen for the 20-year-old sister-in-law, Electa Bryan, and had won her heart. He had left her with a promise to establish himself in a community nearby and marry her in the spring. As a result, he was in Bannack, both to make a fortune in gold and to prove that he could be a good man among good men.

During the winter of 1862-63 the miners burned with the desire to get at the gold in the creeks, but nothing could be done so long as the creeks were frozen. They took to venting their energy at the bar.

Jack Cleveland followed Plummer to Bannack after their term at the Sun River Farm was up, and he quickly became a nuisance. Walking into the Goodrich Hotel one cold winter morning, he blustered that he owned the town of Bannack and would gladly fight anyone who disagreed with him. The remark was directed at Plummer, who was sitting on a bench near the stove, but the gray-eyed man let it pass. Cleveland, who had probably been at the bottle for some time already that day, redirected his energies and began harassing another man about a debt. The debt had long since been paid, but Cleveland caressed his gun in a pointed way nonetheless. When he showed no signs of behaving himself, Plummer turned his steely gaze upon him and told the drunken fool to pipe down. Cleveland complied for a moment, but then renewed his defiance and began shouting insults.

"I'm tired of this," said Plummer and stood up.

No one who met Henry Plummer could dislike him, but some were later seduced into dark suspicions about his true nature. It was rumored that he had come from California because he was running from a bad reputation. Back in Nevada City, it was said, two men had fallen before the barrel of his smoking pistol. Was he a desperado, a fugitive from the law? Beneath his patient, judicious calm lurked a surging power, and Jack Cleveland had gone and provoked it.

Quick as a flash, Plummer drew his gun. He sent one bullet into the ceiling of the hotel and another into one of Cleveland's limbs. Cleveland crashed to his knees and whimpered a plea for mercy. Plummer told him to get up. Cleveland followed the order, but made the mistake of drawing his weapon as he did so. Two more bullets raced into Cleveland's flesh, and he collapsed on the floor. Plummer turned away and later learned that Cleveland had died from his wounds.

Shortly thereafter, Plummer skipped town. Charlie Reeves had got into a fight with the Natives camped south of Bannack, and the bloody end to the dispute had whipped the outraged citizenry into such a level of excitement that Plummer feared a spontaneous reprisal for his killing Jack Cleveland. He had taken the law into his own hands for the third time in his life; what was to stop a keen assailant from doing the same?

Plummer fled towards Rattlesnake Creek in the company of Reeves and two of Reeves's associates. The next morning, their pursuers walked into an ambush, and Plummer negotiated a compromise. The four men would return to Bannack on the condition that they be given a fair trial by the miners' court.

The first criminal trial in Bannack found Henry Plummer innocent of murder. Plummer explained his history with the man whom he had shot. Cleveland had followed him ever since he had left California, because Plummer had been instrumental in sending him to jail once, and Cleveland swore that he would find a way to get even. Having to watch his adversary win the hand of the beautiful Electa Bryan had not sweetened Cleveland's mood. All of Bannack was witness to the threats Cleveland had constantly breathed against Plummer, and when the conflict came to a head, Plummer shot him. The miners determined that Henry Plummer had acted in self-defense.

Reeves and the two other men did not get off so easily. They were found guilty of manslaughter, and would be banished from Bannack as soon as the weather warmed up enough for them to go.

The spring thaw brought glittering success to the life of Henry Plummer. He watched a number of miners hurriedly sift off loose particles of gold and then move on, abandoning their claims because they could not get at the main deposits of gold in the quartz streambed. With the help of the new blacksmith in town, Plummer crafted a little stamping machine, and tried it on the quartz. It rewarded his ingenuity a thousandfold. Gold cascaded from the ore like a stream of sparkling coins, and showered Plummer with riches.

In May 1863, the sheriff of the miners' court resigned his post. He was a surly, sneaking man who had virtually banished himself by pursuing feuds with prominent miners. With a clear majority of the votes, the miners elected Henry Plummer as their new sheriff, and on May 24 Plummer began his duties. It was a little-known fact that the jurisdiction of Bannack had just changed hands, and that the remote boom town was now part of the Territory of Idaho. Most did not notice the shadow of distant laws falling across their sunny valley.

Plummer strode into his new responsibilities with confidence. His own experiences on the wrong side of the law had taught him the need for disinterested justice—for fair and attentive justice, for justice that would collect all the evidence before passing judgment. He knew the crime done a defendant when prosecutors refused to imagine themselves in his position, and he understood the importance of exploring motive and assessing the crime accordingly. Anything less than absolute vigilance with respect to justice would result in irreparable blunders. And if the blunder involved a man going to jail when he had acted in self-defense, it would stain his reputation—not to mention his attitude—forever.

Henry Plummer built the first jail in Bannack. He was devoted to the idea of imprisoning criminals rather than executing them, and solicited subscriptions in the amount of $2.50 from as many people as he could until the detention center was built. He appointed a team of deputies to fan out through the region and help him keep an eye on things. He liked to solve personal disputes himself, and he once bought a horse that a man had used to pay his lawyer, so that the lawyer would not grumble over not having received cash. He tirelessly investigated claims of theft or loss, and even promised a complainant that he would find the bedroll that had been lifted from the man's wagon. But before doing all of this, in June 1863, he married Electa Bryan.

It turned out that being the wife of such a popular and busy sheriff did not suit Electa. When Plummer's jurisdiction was expanded by 80 miles to include Alder Gulch and Virginia City, he was at home less and less often. Electa was forced to spend too much time alone, and even when James Vail abandoned the mission and moved his family south to Bannack, she was not happy. Her exact reasons are shrouded in the mists of time, but history clearly records her decision: she determined to leave Henry to return east. He told her he would settle his affairs in Bannack and then join her.

Plummer rode beside the stage that took Electa south toward Salt Lake City in September 1863. They passed under the mighty Grand Teton peaks on their journey. It was the first and last time that Electa would see them, for after leaving Bannack, she never returned.

At the Snake River crossing, the Plummers met the caravan of the newly appointed chief justice Sidney Edgerton coming the other way. Edgerton, an austere man with suspicious eyes, was traveling to the seat of the new territory in Lewiston, but he never reached it. He found that the mining opportunities at Bannack suited his needs very nicely, and he decided to settle there instead.

All of the Edgertons took a liking to Plummer right off the bat, but as the sheriff of Bannack continued on his way, another

SIDNEY EDGERTON

man at the ferry, a wagon master, spoiled their first impression of their future neighbor. He told them that Plummer was a man with a disreputable past, and that his smiling demeanor was not to be trusted. Edgerton's wife Mary was horrified that the chief lawman of the area was a known desperado; her opinion of him only deteriorated further when she learned that he was a Democrat to boot. Edgerton's ambitious nephew, Wilbur Sanders, who had obediently come west to serve as his uncle's secretary, was also disgusted.

Bannack began to cook when a wave of crime hit the area in late October 1863. Lone miners walking home from the gulches were being mugged. Winning the gold from the stream was only half the battle; getting back to town with your purse and your life intact was just as difficult in these remote areas. Two men held up the Peabody stage near the Rattlesnake ranch, and they bullied the passengers and driver into emptying their pockets. And on a dark night in November, a member of the Edgerton household, Henry Tilden, was stopped by three men wearing blankets and masks up near Horse Prairie Hill. They did not rob him, but his horse got spooked and threw him to the ground. Tilden screamed until help arrived. One of the men, he believed, had been Henry Plummer, who had said that he would be out of town that night to help round up some horses.

"Do not breathe a word of this to anyone," Edgerton warned, after having heard Tilden's story. Plummer was a powerful man in town, and it would take more than a frightened boy's accusations to dislodge him from his high position.

James and Martha Vail threw a party for Thanksgiving, and their brother-in-law ordered a 40-pound turkey and an assortment of expensive wines from Salt Lake City for the occasion. The Edgertons, along with other prominent families of

Bannack, were in attendance and had a good chance to observe their suspect up close. They found his manners somewhat strained. His surface of deception, they determined, was beginning to crack.

One day when Wilbur Sanders was in Alder Gulch on an errand of his uncle's, a grouse hunter burst into the room and announced that he had made a gruesome discovery. He had found the body of Nick Tiebolt, who had been missing for some days. Lariat burns were on his neck, his clothing was ripped ragged, and frozen into his fists were the weeds he had uprooted while being dragged. A bullet hole in the back of his head explained how the torture had ended.

When word got out, the citizens of Alder Gulch were incensed. Someone would have to pay for the murder, and the quicker the better.

Sanders had come to Alder Gulch to enlist support for his Uncle Edgerton's ambition to create a new territory on the eastern slopes of the Rockies with Edgerton as governor. But all thoughts of the political strategy were abandoned when the miners dragged in the prime suspect, one George Ives. With the open sky as their witness, they lit a bonfire, pulled in some wagons for benches and set up their court. Henry Plummer was not present, but his deputy for the area was, and he saw what happened next.

Sanders leapt into the role of prosecutor. This trial would be a showdown between order and crime, he announced, and swore that order would win, no matter what the means. He quickly discovered that Tiebolt had ridden out to Ives's camp to make a payment and had inadvertently displayed a temptingly large quantity of gold dust in his purse. After the transaction, George Ives allegedly watched Tiebolt go and then rode after him with the intent to murder and rob.

The trial lasted three days, but the rising excitement never faltered for a second. When the jury retired to reach a verdict, main street was packed with onlookers. Not one of them would have given up his or her place for the world.

The jury returned. The majority found George Ives guilty of murder. But one man disagreed. This lone juror was not convinced that the crime been adequately explained.

At this point, Wilbur Sanders jumped up on one of the wagons. Should a single voice derail the process of justice? he called out in question. With the force of an avalance exploding forward, the crowd shouted, "No!" Should greedy, guilty George Ives be hanged for his murderous act? he asked. With the joy of releasing an unbearable tension, the crowd shouted, "Yes!" Should Ives's property be seized to pay for the expenses of such a long trial? he asked. The crowd passed this last motion as well, and then surged forward upon their scapegoat. Ives was dragged to the nearest crossbeam, and hurled into space. A nasty knot cut short his fall.

On the night of December 23, 1863, five men gathered in a dark back room of a building in Virginia City, and shook hands. The Vigilance Committee was born. Their oath was loyalty, their means was secrecy and their goal was death.

A number of men soon fell victim to their onslaught, and when they caught a suspicious man named Red Yeager delivering secret messages, they finally got the confession that they wanted to hear. Just before Red Yeager was hanged, he said that the sheriff was the man behind it all. The suspected desperado Henry Plummer was responsible for the crimes.

He was the evil mastermind of the thieves and murderers who were terrorizing the miners of Virginia City and Bannack. *He* was the one who had to die.

The vigilantes did not pause long enough to have their suspicions complicated by opposing views.

On the night of January 10, 1864, the air was clear and cold. Henry Plummer had taken ill, and was resting at the home of his sister-in-law. Suddenly a loud knock came at the door. Martha Vail answered it and was alarmed to find some two dozen men standing outside. A well-known citizen asked for her brother-in-law, and when Plummer heard his name called, he rose and put on his coat. He did not strap on his weapon. Martha anxiously asked what the matter was, and Plummer explained that the men wanted to know the whereabouts of a certain suspected robber. He then left her, and joined the crowd outside.

The company surrounded Plummer and marched him over to Sanders's dwelling. Two of his deputies, Ned Ray and Buck Stinson, walked along side him. Upon reaching Sanders's, the men called softly for their leader, but Sanders had put out his light so that he would not have to face the formidable sheriff. It was then that Plummer realized what was happening. He began speaking in a calm voice, and his words of reason floated into the ears of the men around him like gentle music.

Suddenly Sanders appeared in the doorway. "Company!" he barked. "Forward march!" Recognizing the voice of the shadow, Plummer spun around. Henry's face was illuminated by the moonlight, and his eyes sparkled with a penetrating light.

"Come now," he reasoned mildly to Sanders, "you men know us better than this."

But Sanders looked away.

He again ordered the vigilantes forward, and this time they complied. They herded Plummer and his two deputies out of town, to the very gallows that the successful sheriff Plummer had once helped build, before collecting the funds for his jail.

"Give a man time to pray," Plummer asked. His request was refused. Stinson and Ray were dispatched before him, and he was forced to watch. "Give me a high drop," pleaded Plummer at the last. Instead, he was slowly pulled into the air, and kicked and twitched as the rope tightened. Over a period of some minutes, the implacable rope of the vigilantes strangled him.

Henry Plummer, sheriff of the miners' court of Bannack, suspected fugitive from California, and husband of the beautiful Electa, died without having had a chance to learn the charges against him, or defend himself.

In the first wave of vigilante vengeance, 22 men were lynched. They would go down in history as Henry Plummer's criminal Gang of Innocents—"the Innocents," for short—because each maintained until the end that he was not guilty as charged.

Crime in the gold country of the eastern Rockies only increased after their deaths, and the violent destruction perpetrated by the vigilantes swelled to meet it. One day, though, their reign of terror ended. Sick of the bloodbath, the citizens posted a public notice that all illicit lynchings would be revisited upon the vigilantes in the magnitude of five to one.

Sidney Edgerton went on to become the first governor of the Territory of Montana. Over 70 claims of land rich in the precious elements were registered under his name. Wilber Sanders was no doubt paid handsomely for his obedient service to such a great man.

The town of Bannack fell from prosperity as more and more miners were drawn to the bigger deposits of gold in Alder Gulch and Virginia City. Some time later, it was completely abandoned, and its only inhabitants were the ghosts.

One ghost has wandered long before finally finding rest. The name of the man with the honest, gray-blue eyes would not be cleared of guilt for over a century. 129 years would pass before people asked the right questions about the events leading to that starry mid-winter night, when Sheriff Henry Plummer of Bannack died.

TIBURCIO VASQUEZ

3

Tiburcio Vasquez

Slowly the people backed away from the murdered man, from the murderer, from the pool of dark blood gradually spreading across the wooden floor.

Tiburcio Vasquez, robber, murderer and possibly hero, lived during the gold rush in California. Vasquez has been depicted as a ruthless killer whose victims were usually Easterners lured to California by gold. He has also been described as the brave leader of a people who felt persecuted by the brazen onslaught of whites and the outrageous loss of their homeland. Part opportunist, part hero, he became the lightning rod for Hispanic nationalism in the 1860s and 70s, and for a time he and his gang of bandits operated with impunity, striking stagecoaches and small towns, and then vanishing into the countryside. But what really happens when a single man is vested with the interests of an entire nationality? What, after all, is one wave in the entire mighty sea?

Our story of Tiburcio Vasquez begins when he was not yet 17, in 1852, a time when ethnic tension threatened to explode in California. His pal Anastacio Garcia, a much older man, was deeply concerned about the fate of his people, the Californios, and particularly about the fate of Joaquin Murieta, an outlaw who was then being hunted down by the newly formed California Rangers. On this particular day, they lay on a hillside overlooking the sparkling water below, awaiting the upcoming fandango at the establishment of Jose Guerra. Certain details have been lost to history, but events as they occurred during the remainder of that fateful day may have unfolded as follows.

Tiburcio looked at his older companion. Surely Garcia knew the fandango began at sundown. Why then did they continue to sit here?

"California Rangers," spat Garcia. "The gringos in Sacramento have made a new name for themselves: the California Rangers. Your brother Murieta will not last long now." At Tiburcio's silence, Anastacio Garcia pushed the hat from his forehead and sat up. "Your brother Murieta will not escape the California Rangers. Is that of so little consequence to you? Have you no sense of honor? Have you no loyalty to your people?"

Tiburcio started under the stinging lash of the last words.

"He is not my brother," said Tiburcio and stood up.

"He *is* your brother," retorted Garcia, who also rose and surveyed the young man. "You do not understand these things. We are losing our struggle. Every year, more gringos come to this land that was once ours. The old *pueblos* are nothing compared to the new cities. Foreigners come here and get rich by stealing gold from beneath the very foundation of our houses! And what do our people do? They can do nothing but watch. You remember this: without them your freedom means nothing. Your freedom is a drop in this ocean! And if the ocean dries up, your freedom dries up with it."

Garcia's harshness faded and he turned towards the horses. Tiburcio quickly gathered up their things. Garcia swung astride his horse and with an exaggerated flourish announced their destination to the sky. "To the *dancehall*," he proclaimed, and started down the hill. Tiburcio scrambled to follow him. Garcia had uttered the last word in English.

Upon reaching Monterey—Tiburcio Vasquez's birthplace— they slipped inconspicuously through the streets to Jose Guerra's establishment. A Mexican flag was flapping in the stiff breeze; the lights were on and the music was playing. Tiburcio tied up his horse beside Garcia's, and followed him through the crowd and into the party. He drifted happily up to the bar, where he found himself once more beside Garcia.

Garcia and the proprietor exchanged pleasantries as a bottle and two glasses slid into position in front of the men.

A small, anxious-looking man bustled officiously through the crowd, demanding that the festive sea part for him. "Señor Guerra! Señor Guerra!" he called.

"Well, Ramón, what is it?" asked Guerra when the man reached the bar.

"Constable Hardimont!" he hissed. "He is coming up the street!"

"Alright," Guerra responded. "Stop the music. And take the flag down."

Ramón nodded and turned to go. Garcia stopped him.

"No," he said quietly, taking hold of Ramón's sleeve. "Leave the flag up."

"Anastacio," Guerra warned. "Don't cause any trouble here."

"Let me go," squealed Ramón. Then he added, "If I were you, I'd worry a little about what the constable will do when he finds a dirty bandit hanging around in a public place."

Garcia's eyes narrowed. "What did you call me?"

"Let me go!" cried Ramón. He suddenly shoved his tormentor, causing Garcia to fall back from his stool and spill his drink on himself.

Garcia did not let go of Ramón, and when he regained his balance, he lunged and bent the quivering man to the ground. "You are *not* going to take down that flag!" he seethed. "You are *not* going to let a damn gringo ruin our party! And I am *not* going to let you go!" He paused, then brutally struck Ramón on the head.

By this time, Guerra had flitted around the bar and yanked Garcia away from Ramón. Garcia writhed around. Madness was in his eyes.

"Traitor!" he cursed. "Cowardly traitor! Traitor to the gringos!" The two men crashed to the ground, locked in furious combat as the crowd surged around them.

Tiburcio suddenly saw a new commotion at the door. Constable Hardimont had arrived. The moment could not have been worse. People were trying to block his entry into the dark hall, but the resistance apparently only steeled the lawman's intention to search out the cause of the disorder.

"Where is the proprietor?" he roared. The people gave way, and he strode into their midst. Suddenly Tiburcio was before him.

"Sir," he explained in English, "There was a slight misunderstanding, that is all, and unfortunately-"

"Move aside, boy," Hardimont ordered, brushing Tiburcio out of his way. He broke into the circle surrounding the fight, pulled Guerra from the fray and shook him. Garcia stumbled away.

Guerra's chest was still heaving when, in a deliberately low voice, he began to explain. "Constable, I apologize. I can explain. The flag... I know nothing about the flag. And the incident here was an accident—" He was not given a chance to finish; a dark shape sprang forward, and, with the momentum of a locomotive, plunged a flashing blade into the side of Constable William Hardimont. The attacker ducked away. The constable was half dead before he realized what had happened. His hands grew limp; he slumped to the ground, then lay still. Gasping with terror, Guerra leapt away from the body.

Not six feet from him stood Garcia, frozen in a position of deadly aggression. The knife was still in his hand.

Silence fell over the crowd. Slowly the people backed away from the murdered man, from the murderer, from the pool of dark blood gradually spreading across the wooden floor. Their eyes held the assailant in place.

The crowd ebbed out of the hall. Tiburcio, Guerra and Garcia were left alone.

"Garcia," croaked Guerra. "What have you done?" His gaze had been locked on the body of the constable, but he broke it to look down at his trousers, and saw that they were covered with the dead man's blood.

Garcia lowered the knife, and his gaze met Tiburcio's. For a moment, Tiburcio glimpsed a pleading fear in his friend's eyes. But then Garcia's face became a mask. The cheeks looked numb, the eyes were opaque, the mouth jaded.

"Run, Tiburcio," the man said, snapping the silence.

The day after the stabbing of Constable William Hardimont, a grim bunch of white vigilantes descended on the dancehall of Jose Guerra, where they found Guerra's clothes stained with the constable's blood. They threw a rope around Guerra's neck, hauled him into the air and left him swinging as an example of what would happen to those who were suspected of stabbing whites. Before long, Anastacio Garcia had also been tracked down. He too dangled at the end of a rope when revenge had run its course. When it was whispered that Tiburcio Vasquez had been named as an associate of Garcia's, the young man did not wait to argue with the vigilantes. He took the advice given him by his late mentor, and ran.

The city from which he fled had been established by his people in 1770. These people were the Californios, colonists of Spanish or Mexican descent, who had lived in loose political affiliation with the central government in Mexico since the 1820s. Their economy was largely rural. After the routing of Mexico by Americans during the Mexican War in the 1840s the Californios suddenly found that they too were Americans, despite their language and ethnic distinctiveness. New Mexico, Colorado, Utah, Arizona and

CENTRAL CALIFORNIA

Nevada were also ceded to the United States in the Treaty of Guadalupe Hidalgo, which settled the war. Although California did not officially enter the Union until 1850, white newcomers from the East were already streaming into California during the 1840s. The flow increased dramatically when gold was discovered near Coloma by James Marshall, who had been contracted to build a mill for the landowner John Sutter. The gold rush ran roughshod over the Californios. Their relatively quiet and peaceful ranching existence was soon overwhelmed by the gold-hungry hordes. The establishment of instant towns—shanties and shacks thrown up overnight, complete with saloon, dance hall, dry-goods store and brothel—completely changed their way of life. The Californios reacted as expected to the unstoppable intrusion: they either slipped into despair or seethed with bitterness.

Vasquez was no guerrilla leader, but his free-wheeling opportunism did seem to align itself with the ethnic fault line in California. Shocked by the deaths of Guerra and Garcia, and too afraid to return home, he drifted east and fell in with a band of horse rustlers; but these men were also caught and lynched by vigilantes, and Tiburcio was forced to keep running. His initial experience taught him that Californios were to be trusted, and whites were not. He would later decide that the only one he could really rely on was himself.

Some time after the death of Constable Hardimont, Tiburcio Vasquez risked a visit to his mother. According to his account, he asked for her blessing on his determination to venture out into the world and live off it in whatever way he could.

In 1857, he was arrested in Los Angeles for horse rustling. The trial did much to sour Vasquez's belief in other human beings. He had been arrested with an old friend, and the two plotted to slant their testimony, each to the other's favor. When their day in court arrived, however, Vasquez got a nasty surprise. His *amigo* had turned State's evidence to rescue himself. Vasquez was fully blamed for the crime and went to the slammer alone. On August 1857, he entered the prison of San Quentin. He escaped in the general jailbreak of 1859, but was recaptured within two months and served out his sentence until August 1863.

Within a year of his release, Vasquez was embroiled in the murder of an Italian butcher at the Enriquita mine. In order to get testimony from the Spanish-speaking miners, the inquest enlisted the help of Vasquez, the only fluently bilingual man at the mine. The process failed to come up with any useful testimony and did not lead to a single arrest. Having completed his obligation, Vasquez moved on; a little while later, the authorities learned that there had in fact been no shortage of decisive testimony. Something, it seemed, had been lost in the translation.

Vasquez was caught stealing cattle in 1866. This time, his soujourn in San Quentin lasted from January 1867 until the summer of 1870. After his release, his activities on the shady side of the law resumed with wild abandon.

With a man named Francisco Bassinez, he was taken in by an old aquaintance named Abelardo Salazar. Vasquez returned the hospitality by luring Salazar's young wife away and seducing her, after which he apparently tired of her and "gave" her to Bassinez. The outraged husband chanced upon Vasquez some time later and, as sometimes happens in these circumstances, shot him. Vasquez took the bullet in the neck but somehow lived.

He fled to Cantua Canyon, which lies east of San Francisco in the shadow of Mount Diablo. The destination was not insignificant: the canyon had been the hideout of the legendary Joaquín Murieta, the notorious (but perhaps fictitious) badman whose fate so concerned Garcia back on the hillside in 1852, and whose resistance to white settlers had allegedly ended in a gruesome decapitation at the hands of the ruthless California Rangers. In his present state of urgency, Vasquez discovered that the canyon suited his needs quite well.

In the spring of 1871, he rode out from his camp with Bassinez and another man named Narcisso Rodriguez. The three men held up the Visalia stagecoach at Soap Lake near Hollister. No blood was shed, but the driver and passengers were tied up and left exposed in the hot sun until help arrived. Pursued, the bandits were overtaken near Santa Cruz. Bassinez died in the skirmish, but Rodriguez was caught alive and was later brought before a jury. Vasquez again suffered a near mortal injury—one account states that a bullet entered his chest and lodged itself under his shoulder blade—but he fought on and shot the lawman who had wounded him. He then flung himself upon his horse and wearily rode back to his Cantua hideout, where he spent several weeks recovering.

Tiburcio Vasquez may have journeyed to Mexico after the Soap Lake holdup, but if he did, he did not stay long. Nowhere was he more secure than in the Cantua Canyon, where he was supported and even admired. He attracted a gang of willing bandits. Abdon Leiva, August "the humpbacked Frenchman" DeBert, Teodoro Moreno, Romulo Gonzalez and Cleovaro Chavez all read a sort of messianic nationalism into Vasquez's lawless opportunism, and their power swelled when they cooperated. Furthermore, they were protected by the sea of Californio ranches, into which they could disappear at will when threatened by white lawmen.

Emboldened by a successful raid on Firebaugh's Ferry and looking for a better payoff, Vasquez and Chavez decided to move on to bigger targets. Chavez had become somewhat of a lieutenant to Vasquez by introducing more sophisticated strategy to the gang, and he convinced Vasquez that the returns from holding up general stores and lone stagecoaches would pale compared to the rewards of train robbery.

In the spring of 1873, they set a course for an exposed stretch of the Southern Pacific Railroad between San Jose and Gilroy. Their plan was to tear up a section of the track in order to derail a substantial shipment of money. While underway, however, they were forced to abandon the idea. Apparently, the inconceivable had happened: someone among their aquaintances had informed the railroad authorities in San Francisco of their intentions. The train was postponed. Frustrated, the bandits hit a supply station instead, and robbed it of $200.

The next holdup occurred August 26, 1873 at a little town about 50 miles east of Monterey called Tres Pinos.

The clerk at Snyder's store, John Utzerath, had just served Leiva and Gonzalez another round of drinks and cigars when Moreno entered brandishing a pistol. The three outlaws ordered everyone in the store—including a blacksmith named L.C. Smith—to stand against the bar, where they were bound hand and foot. The robbers searched their victims for money and valuables. Thereafter, Chavez and Vasquez arrived. Vasquez ordered his men also to take whatever food and supplies they could find, and then returned outside. He was in time to find a Portuguese shepherd approaching. Vasquez, who was armed with both a pistol and a rifle, ordered the shepherd to remain where he was. The man did not understand him, and realized too late the import of the command. He saw the weapons and turned to run. After hearing Vasquez's order, one of the bandits, either Gonzalez or Moreno, joined Vasquez. The shepherd was murdered while trying to get over a fence; whether the bullet that shattered his skull came from Vasquez's gun or Moreno's is not precisely known. In the confusion, the young son of L.C. Smith tried to make a break for it. He was tripped by Chavez and bludgeoned unconscious.

Then another innocent man stumbled onto the scene. George Redford, a teamster, drove his team up to the store, and was climbing down from the wagon when Vasquez barked out an order to lie down. Redford was deaf, but he too understood the gist of the command without understanding its words. He bolted for the stable. Vasquez gunned him down before he could escape. The owner of the hotel, Leander Davidson, witnessed the execution. Vasquez spun to find him scurrying for cover. At this point, Abdon Leiva came out of the store to find out what had gone wrong. He yelled out to Davidson that if he shut and locked his door, no one would get hurt. He was interrupted by another murderous blast from Vasquez's rifle. While still fumbling with the bolt, Davidson suffered a shot to the chest; he fell dead into the arms of his horrified wife. Another teamster pulled up, unaware of the robbery going on. Vasquez walked over to him and gave him a cruel blow to the head.

Inside the store, the ambitious robbery was almost complete. Vasquez entered and dragged the owner, Andrew Snyder, into the back room, where Snyder was forced to reveal and relinquish all the cash and jewelry he had. Having obtained everything of value that could be taken, the robbers leisurely rode out of town. The robbery had lasted over three hours. Three people were dead, two lay unconscious, a number were tied up helpless—and many more would be terrified, when news of the Tres Pinos massacre reached them.

The bandits' escape was complicated by a romantic event. Vasquez might have saved himself a good deal of trouble had he kept his hands off Rosaria Leiva, the wife of Abdon. After splitting off from Moreno and Gonzalez, Vasquez, Leiva and Chavez had ridden on to a ranch, where Leiva's family was waiting for him. The enlarged party then camped at Rock Creek, and it was there that Leiva caught Vasquez with his wife. At first Leiva demanded a duel. After some consideration, he opted for a more damaging plan. Taking his family with him, he turned back to give himself up. Ironically, the pursuing posse led by Sheriff Adams missed him, but he soon arrived at a nearby station. There he turned himself in to await the return of the sheriff. Adams came close to pinning Vasquez and Chavez in Rock Creek Canyon, but his posse scattered when the outlaws surprised them with heavy gunfire, and because Vasquez and Chavez had the fresher horses, they easily escaped. The news that Leiva was willing to turn State's evidence could not have come at a better time for the sheriff. His interview of Leiva led directly to the capture, trial and sentencing of Teodoro Moreno. Moreno was found guilty of the murder of Bernal Berhuri, the Portuguese shepherd, and though he escaped the noose, he was to spend the rest of his life in jail.

In December of the same year, the Vasquez Gang swooped into Kingston in Fresno County and held the entire population hostage. Thirty-five men were tied up helpless. The citizens were terrorized by the bandits, who made off with over $2000 in cash and valuables. Some accounts state that Vasquez lingered outside of town until his men had finished the work. The brazen raid, coupled with the killings at Tres Pinos, prompted Governor Newton Booth to issue wanted posters bearing the likeness of Tiburcio Vasquez and to offer an $8000 reward for the capture of the notorious bandit.

The increased pressure had little immediate effect. In February 1874, the bandits surrounded the stagecoach depot at Coyote Hole Station and robbed the Owens and Los Angeles stagecoach. The next day, while making their escape through Soledad Canyon, the bandits ran into another stagecoach, and robbed it as well. They did not rob the second stagecoach for money. Nor did they require food. They would have left fewer traces of their passage if they had not robbed it all.

While the Vasquez Gang seemed to jump out from nowhere and slip away like fish in the sea, a sheriff named Morse in Alameda county was slowly but surely gathering knowledge of its ways and habits, and of other, less well-known bandits. He heard of the latest holdups, and added the accounts to his collection. Over time, his single-minded persistence, personal bravery and relentless pursuit would strike the same measure of fear into the bandits as they inflicted on the populace. Sheriff Morse studied the Vasquez Gang exhaustively. His best move was to ingratiate himself with not only white but also Californio ranchers throughout south-central California. Along with Sheriff William Rowland of Los Angeles, he was dedicated to bringing Vasquez to justice.

The effectiveness of Morse's work and the reduction of criminal activity was not lost on Governor Booth. In March 1874, following raids at Havilah and Soledad Canyon by Vasquez and his outlaws, Booth convinced the state legislature to apportion $5000 to the outfitting and funding of Morse and a select team of crack bounty hunters. Their sole purpose would be to put an end to the string of robberies by capturing the crook alive.

At the end of the winter rainy season, Morse led his men into the mountains. In two months, from mid-March to the middle of May, the party of lawmen covered an incredible expanse of inhospitable territory in their hunt for the elusive bandit leader. They rode over 2700 miles through wild and difficult country. Forests, flatlands, scrub brush, semi-arid steppes, deserts: no terrain kept them from their purpose. The bounty hunters endured long hours in the saddle. They slept at night in the waning warmth of campfire embers high in the Santa Lucia or San Rafael ranges. They sweat under a blazing sun while battling scrub brush. They wound their way single file through deep canyons and narrow ravines. In spite of their efforts to surprise their adversary unawares, Vasquez and his band of outlaws remained at large.

Meanwhile, Vasquez and his men pulled off an extraordinary robbery at a ranch near the San Gabriel mission. They pretended to be sheep shearers, but pulled out pistols when they had the rancher alone, and demanded his money. When the rancher, Alexander Repetto, claimed to have only $80, Vasquez angrily stated that he knew about Repetto's recent sale of livestock, which had apparently brought Repetto over $10,000. Repetto protested that the money had already been used to buy up land and pay debts, upon which Vasquez demanded to see the accounts and bills of sale. So as the gang members twiddled their thumbs outside for what seemed hours, Vasquez and Repetto pored over the ledgers like two accountants, until at last the bandit satisfied himself that Repetto was mostly telling the truth. Vasquez then complimented him on his honesty, explained that he would nevertheless need a small sum of money to cover the needs of his men (the needs exceeded the $80 Repetto claimed to have), and promised to make repayment with interest after 30 days. Not in a position to refuse, Repetto sent a boy to Los Angeles with a check for $800. Suspicions were aroused at the bank, however, and Sheriff Rowland questioned the boy. Convinced that Vasquez was at Repetto's, Rowland quickly formed a posse and rode out to apprehend the wanted criminal. But the alarm was sounded in time and Vasquez escaped.

The $8000 reward for the capture of Tiburcio Vasquez might have been scorned by the Californios when it was first advertised on the posters that carried the face of their outlaw hero, but that initial scorn did not eliminate the offer. Each day, the $8000 was offered, and each day it went unclaimed. Every hour increased its allure. It was only a matter of time before someone would put acute personal need before vague nationalistic duty.

At Fort Tejon, Sheriff Morse was informed that Vasquez was holed up at the ranch of a man known as Greek George, at the foot of the mountains 10 miles west of Los Angeles. Morse relayed the information to Rowland, who, after hesitating because of doubt about the informant's reliability, followed it up. On May 13, 1874, Rowland assembled some lawmen and approached Greek George's ranch by a circuitous, little-used road that afforded the party an unobserved approach. In the early dawn hours of the next day, a Mexican wagon team was seen heading for the ranch. Rowland commandeered it and, on threat of death to the teamsters if they raised an alarm, had his men ride prone in the wagon until they were nearly at the entrance. Then the lawmen jumped out, rifles at the ready, and surrounded the house. Vasquez was in the middle of a meal.

The wife of Greek George caught sight of the lawmen from the front door, and shouted out a warning to Vasquez. As the posse barged into the kitchen, the desperate bandit leader leapt for an open window. As he did so, one of the lawmen fired his shotgun at the fleeing figure, wounding Vasquez with buckshot. Vasquez rolled into a courtyard and turned to bolt for his horse, but shots being fired from all directions convinced him of the hopelessness of his situation. Blood streaming from his left leg, side and shoulder, the terror of central California raised his hands and surrendered to the lawmen. Vasquez was laid on a pallet and transported to the Los Angeles jail. He said nothing during the trip.

After a brief stay in Los Angeles, Vasquez was sent to San Jose to stand trial for murder and armed robbery. His trial began on January 5, 1875, and was attended by the elite of San Jose. White citizens from Monterey who still remembered Constable Hardimont came to see the last of his murderers sentenced. The local paper indignantly reported that a large number of women attended the trial because they were attracted to the ruthless Vasquez. Finally, upstanding Californio citizens filled in the remaining space in the courtroom where much more than the fate of a single man would be decided. The people jostled and mingled, and the sound of their voices washed over the prisoner's mind like the noise of waves.

The bandit had appealed to the Californio community for defense funds and was able to hire two attorneys. They argued the case to the best of their ability, but the prosecution called Abdon Leiva to the stand, who testified that he had watched Tiburcio Vasquez kill Leander Davidson on August 26, 1873. Nervous that chaos would erupt when the jury returned, the judge demanded silence in the courtroom, and stated that anyone who opened his mouth in response to the verdict would be immediately arrested.

The jury returned. It had found the defendant guilty of murder. Beckoning Vasquez to leave the prisoner's box and advance before the court, the judge sentenced him to death.

Vasquez's lawyers were directed to launch an appeal, which they promptly did. At the same time, a letter was found stuffed into the mailbox of the Wells Fargo Express Company in Hollister. It spoke to the worst of the white settlers' fears. Purportedly written by Vasquez's lieutenant Chavez, the letter warned that the Californios would not accept the death of their rebel hero. The letter stated that Chavez was roaming the mountains with the other gang members—some feared as many as 200—who had not been captured in the raid. They intended to rescue the man whose name had become synonymous with Californio resistance, and swore that only death would keep them from their goal. Moreover, the letter threatened malicious and uncontrollable vengeance should Vasquez be hanged. The letter further threatened that the white citizens would "have to suffer as in the times of Joaquín Murieta," and that "the just and the unjust alike" would be the victims of Californio revenge. Officials dismissed the letter as a hoax. There was no evidence that Chavez could even write. Whether or not the script was authentic, was of little consequence; in the minds of the white citizens of coastal California, the words carried the weight of a tidal wave.

The final appeal for the doomed bandit was dismissed on March 12, 1875, and the hanging scheduled for exactly one week later. The city of San Jose had no gallows, so the sheriff borrowed one from the state capitol in Sacramento. Invitations to lawmen and leading citizens were issued and Sheriff Adams of Santa Clara County distributed Vasquez's last two letters to the newspapers for publication. The first apologized to all he had harmed in the course of his long career of crime; the second was an appeal to his compatriots still at large. Ever the leader, Vasquez urged them to repent of their ways and take up honest professions, writing that he did not want them to face the same fate as he.

The hanging was scheduled for 1:30 PM inside the bounds of the courthouse. The public was barred from the event, but by dawn a large crowd was already assembling in front of the courthouse.

Shortly after one o'clock, Sheriff Adams read the death warrant to the condemned man and then announced sternly that the time had come. Nothing came of the letter allegedly written by Chavez; Tiburcio Vasquez remained in his cell until the hangman came and got him. No rhetoric of resistance or race stood by him in the final moment. When death came, he faced it alone.

The bandit stood up and followed the guards and the sheriff to the gallows, accompanied by the local priest. Vasquez took his place on the trap door beside the rope. Thirteen years before, Anastacio Garcia had contemplated a similar loop of cord. But he was gone now, as was Guerra, Bassinez, Gonzalez and Moreno. A final religious ceremony took place. The wind had picked up speed. The executioner slipped the rope around Vasquez's neck. All voices were muted as the noose was adjusted; only Vasquez was heard, as he hissed to the hangman, "*Pronto!*"

The trap was sprung. Vasquez plummeted toward the ground, but was jerked to a halt before reaching it. The scourge of California was pronounced dead seven minutes later. He turned slowly in midair as the small group of spectators filed out of the courtyard.

JOHN WESLEY HARDIN

4

John Wesley Hardin

Suddenly someone screamed out a warning.
Hardin whirled and cross-drew in one
fluid motion, his guns blazing.

After the Civil War ended in 1865, reconciliation between the North and South was thwarted by continuing conflict. The battles had not all been won, or lost. Until 1877, the government in Washington pursued its program of Reconstruction in the defeated Confederacy, but met with resistance at almost every turn. On the one side were the hardline Northerners, or Radicals, who wanted radical change in the South. They demanded a total abolition of the racist inequality upon which the economy of the South had been based, and took away the basic citizenship of all former Confederate soldiers and powerful landowners. On the other side were the conservative Southerners, who resented their once-thriving culture being overrun by greedy carpetbaggers. War had become a way of life by 1865, and taking up arms to solve a dispute had long been the way of the frontier. In Texas, a few gunmen emerged as violent rebels against Reconstruction and Republican (Northern) rule. Among them, one lone figure stands out. Though he was no politician, his murderous career rode the wave of political discontent, and has become a symbol for the aftermath of the Civil War.

John Wesley Hardin was the fastest draw in Reconstruction Texas. A certain alertness marked his actions, and his deft assurance in action seemed the result of a keen perception of the world around him. But from the very first, he felt that everyone was against him. His golden rule was self-preservation, and he viewed others' statements as hostile challenges. The Wild West was an arena of glory, and Hardin's expert gunfights masked what today might be diagnosed as psychopathy: he showed neither remorse nor regret, and was full of self-centered contradictions. He was, in short, a cold-blooded killer.

He was born in Bonham, Texas on May 26, 1853, into a distinguished family. One great-uncle had fought in the battle of San Jacinto (1836), in which Texas won freedom from Mexico. Another had been a signatory to the Texas Declaration of Independence. His grandfather had served with considerable distinction in the Congress of Texas. His father was a Methodist preacher who also taught and practiced law as circumstances demanded. His father had named this second son after the founder of Methodism in hopes that the boy would grow up to join the ministry.

His father was wrong.

The first hint at young John Wesley's future occurred early, some time after the young family had resettled in southeastern Texas, in Polk County. He got into a fight at school with a classmate over a girl. The other boy had teased the girl, and when John Wesley came to her defense, the argument got heated. Both boys pulled knives. The other boy may have moved first, but John Wesley moved faster. He thrust forward and stabbed his antagonist deep in the chest. As his opponent fell, he sprang back and then attacked again, slicing the back of the fallen boy. Girls in the circle screamed, and the boys jumped back, afraid of the look on John Wesley's face. Hardin glowered, pocketed the knife and turned away. He was 11 years old.

The boy did not die, and Hardin's attack was excused as self-defense and protection of the weaker sex. He continued to attend the school, but his interest lay in guns. In his free time, he made models of Abraham Lincoln and used them for target practice.

In April 1865, word came to southeastern Texas that the Confederate Army had been defeated. The surviving soldiers trickled home. Desolation was etched into their faces; tattered gray uniforms hung from their bones. Soon they were followed by the bluecoats of the North. The war was officially over, but battles continued to burn throughout the Texas countryside. President Andrew Johnson announced that the rebellion had been quelled everywhere but Texas; in July 1867, Texas was put under military rule.

John Wesley Hardin sealed his own fate when he killed a man in the fall of 1868. He was visiting at his uncle's plantation when it happened. He and his cousin challenged the man, whose name was Mage, to a wrestling match. Mage had been the slave of a local farmer and was now working for Hardin's uncle. What began as fun quickly soured. Hardin scratched Mage in the face during the roughhousing. Mage stumbled back, touched his hand to the scratch, and saw red.

He cursed the youngster, and threatened to beat him senseless. Hardin backed off.

He told his uncle about the incident, and his uncle advised him to pack up his things and head home. Under the military regime, picking fights with a black man was not a good idea.

But the next day, as Hardin was riding out, the tall stalks of sugar cane at the side of the road parted, and Mage stepped out onto the road in front of him. It seemed a rematch was in order, but this time the young man packed a glinting pistol. Mage advanced towards him with a heavy stick. Hardin warned him off, and drew his gun. Whether the confusion of the moment caused Mage to pause or falter is not known. The gun jumped in Hardin's hands. Once. Twice. Three times. Three point-blank shots cracked into Mage's chest. The wounded man collapsed onto the ground.

Life lingered in Mage for a few days, but the wounds were fatal. He died, and with him died the Hardins' hopes for their son. All thoughts of a fair trial—one that would favor a verdict of self-defense—were dismissed. By killing a black man, Hardin had become not only a murderer, but also an unrepentant Confederate rebel.

Perhaps it had been an accident. But it was the wrong time for accidents of that kind. John Wesley Hardin had taken the first step on the path to being a wanted criminal, not to mention the most "unreconstructed" gunman in the Lone Star State.

When Union soldiers rode up to the farmhouse where Hardin was hiding out, he did not waste time ascertaining their intent. They were surprised by his ambush, and all three fell before the barrel of his gun.

He fled northwest to Corsicana, where his father's influence got him a job in the small community school. He made no secret of his past, but the killing of a few bluecoats was hardly condemned by the people in whose midst he lived. His father still vested some hope in his second son, and believed he would prove good.

Hardin found his calling, however, when he threw over teaching school in favor of the life of the cowboy. Corsicana was a lively town, and Hardin shot his way into fame with the dexterous control of his pistols at work and at play. He fell in with roughriders and wranglers, and took to hanging around the saloons and racetracks. Outright flaunting of Republican rule earned him respect from the men around him and looks from the ladies. Power swelled in him. When his father met him in Towash in December 1869 to tell John Wesley that the family had moved up to Corsicana so that they could all be together again, he was beyond reclaiming.

On Christmas Day in 1869, the one-room box house that served as a gambling palace in Towash, Texas, was full of gamblers, whores and cowboys. Hardin sat at the main table, playing poker with a few other men, his nimble hands floating cards into neat piles on the grimy table. A blue smoke hung in the air. Hardin had been winning steadily, beating a rough-hewn local named Bradly round after round. Suddenly a long blade flashed in Bradly's hand. His chair clattered to the floor as he rose.

"That money is mine, you little cheat," Bradly blustered.

Hardin could only watch as Bradly stole back all his winnings; because the game had been friendly up to that point, he had taken off his holster and his boots, and laid them in the corner. He looked over to the corner now. His possessions were gone.

"Beat it, kid," snarled Bradly. Hardin backed out the door into the frosty night. Bradly laughed. He had bullied the notorious 16-year-old at cards, tricked him out of his gun, and forced him to run away without his boots.

A short while later, a stranger entered and said he had been sent by Hardin to ask for his possessions back. Bradly threw the boots to him, and told him to get out. Later another man came in, and requested Hardin's pistol on behalf of its owner. Bradly jumped up angrily.

"I suppose I'll have to kill that fool boy," he muttered and stormed outside. There in the moonlit street stood a ghostly silhouette. He was armed. Surprised by the sudden confrontation, Bradly fumbled for his weapon and managed to get off an awkward shot before he was hit. One bullet blew off the top of Bradly's head. A second plugged his chest and exited through a fist-sized hole in his back. He crashed to the cold ground, bounced off his side and landed on his back. Only then did the blood spread over his shirt. Brains and unrecognizable gore were splattered around him. His eyes stared up into the starry Texas night.

John Wesley Hardin turned away, and receded into the night. Word soon spread that he possessed the fastest draw in Texas.

Time and again, he proved the rumors true. One killing led to another, as Hardin fled from town to town. He shot a circus worker dead in Horn Hill, Texas, when the burly man threatened to fight him. A week later, Hardin fell prey to a well-practiced ruse. A woman approached him and pretended to take a fancy to him. Suddenly, her boyfriend showed up and demanded Hardin's money in return for having insulted his girl. Usually the victim of this ruse would stammer out an embarrassed apology and comply, but this time, the robbers had picked on the wrong man. Hardin purposely dropped some of the money as he was handing it over, and shot the man in the head as the latter was bending to pick it up.

Hardin settled for a time on the farm of an uncle near Brenham, but the peace did not last long. On March 20, 1870, the military occupation officially ended, and Texas was readmitted to the United States of America with the Republican E.J. Davis as its governor. The state was by no means free of confusion and bloodshed, however. Governor Davis promptly replaced the retreating bluecoats with his own racially diverse state police force. The ethnic composition of the police force caused pugnacious rebels like John Wesley Hardin to dub the new government "Negro rule." Moreover, a new sort of rebellion had arisen alongside that of the traditional gunslingers; this crew walked at night under the yellow light of burning crosses, and they wore ghostly white hoods to mask their seething desire for revenge.

The exact number of state policemen whom John Wesley Hardin killed is not known, but they were by his own account his prime enemies. Most of what is known about Hardin comes from a late autobiography and partisan accounts written by supporters. These histories probably exaggerate the number of policemen shot down by Hardin, but the point of their bloody descriptions of murder after "necessary" murder is clear. While most of Texas began to accept the new face of order—albeit slowly, given that the police could be as brutal as the rebels—Hardin and the Klu Klux Klan did not.

State policemen caught up with Hardin in Marshall, Texas. He was jailed briefly while his identity was in question (he seemed too young to be the notorious killer), and then he was tied to a horse for transfer to Waco. Foolishly, his captors failed to search him again after taking him out of his cell. The party stopped one night at a farmhouse to ask directions. As soon as he was left alone with only one guard, Hardin somehow managed to extricate a pistol that someone had slipped him in prison. He killed the guard and escaped before the others could return.

In January 1871, he moved south into Gonzalez County. His plan was to cross the Rio Grande into Mexico, but he was welcomed by relatives whose surname was Clements, and they convinced him to stay. It was there that he met Jane Bowen, his future bride. He also became embroiled in the Sutton-Taylor feud, a sort of extension of the Civil War that pitted the rebellious Confederate family of Creek Taylor against a marauding party of ex-lawmen led by Jack Helm and William E. Sutton. Helm's and Sutton's men called themselves "the Regulators." Hardin decided that he was not one to be regulated, and gradually aligned himself with the Taylor faction.

Thousands of Texas ranchers drove their cattle up the Chisolm Trail to Abilene, Kansas in 1871. The event interrupted Hardin's life in Gonzalez. He left both feud and future wife to help his cousins Manning and Jim Clements take their cattle north. The cattle drive was by all accounts a historic event, and Hardin used every opportunity to show that he was as much a cowboy as the next man. Officials in Texas and Kansas, including the famous lawman Wild Bill Hickok, heard of Hardin's exploits, but could not intervene, at least not until the 1000-mile-long human chain of the West's toughest men had dissolved again. Hardin rode with his cousins from their ranch near the Guadelupe River to Kansas, delivered the herd, and got paid for his efforts. He stayed on to paint the town red. Hardin conspicuously disobeyed Marshal Hickok's order not to carry guns in public while he was in Kansas. A standoff between the two marksmen may well have occurred, but neither fell before the other's gun.

After returning to Gonzales County, in March 1872 Hardin and his beloved Jane Bowen went to a Methodist preacher and tied the knot. She knew all about his violent history, but explained it according to the politics of the time: in her mind, Hardin was justified in his resistance of Republican rule.

The outlaw was soon in trouble again. Some ranching business took him up towards the Louisiana border, and on his way home he stopped off in Trinity, Polk County, the heart of Hardin country. He and a cousin—Barnett Jones, the very same cousin with whom he had wrestled the freed man Mage four years previously—played some of the locals at tenpins. A gunman named Phil Sublett watched Hardin lose round after round, and then suggested a match between the two of them with five dollars at stake for each game. Hardin agreed and quickly rattled off six straight games, gloating as he raked in his winnings. Sublett realized that he had been had, and angrily departed. He returned a short time later with a rifle. Having spotted Hardin from the doorway, he raised the rifle and fired. Glass shattered, wood exploded and patrons dived for cover. Hardin took the buckshot in his left hip. He drew his pistols and staggered after Sublett, blood running down his legs. The coward was escaping up the road. Hardin shot him in the back and then pitched face first into the street.

"I'm done for," he moaned.

Had he been in any other town, he would have been right. Relatives came to the rescue when almost anybody else would have left him to die. They dragged him from the dusty street and spirited him off to the physician's office, where the bullets were removed without an anaesthetic.

Word quickly reached the state police that Hardin was vulnerable, and they tracked him. Supporters rushed him from hiding place to hiding place, but the police caught up to him at a farmhouse in Angelina County. Hardin took another shot in the leg before driving off the attackers with the deadly accuracy of his shotgun.

How exactly did John Wesley Hardin find the time to recover from near-fatal shotgun wounds, and still escape the relentless state police? One version of the story explains that he turned himself in to a sheriff whom he could trust and was transferred by four state policemen back to Gonzalez, where he recuperated in jail not far from his pregnant wife. The policemen were allegedly told not to harm the popular rebel during the journey, because an election was at hand, and Governor Davis could not afford to lose a single supporter. When he had recovered, a friend gave him a little file, and he sawed his way to freedom. If the story is true, then John Wesley Hardin must have led a charmed life.

Two little miracles broke the charm.

The first was a daughter. On February 6, 1873, Jane Hardin gave birth to a their first child. They named her Mary Elizabeth, or Molly for short. John Wesley Hardin had become a father and, whether he liked it or not, all future fights and flights would necessarily include his family.

The second was a vote. A new legislature had just been elected, and it was overwhelmingly composed of Democrats. In April 1873, they repealed Governor Davis's police law and sacked the state police force. Governor Davis himself would soon be replaced by a Democrat. Republicanism and Reconstruction no longer ruled Texas. The upshot was that John Wesley Hardin could no longer justify his violence as political resistance.

Unfortunately, murder was like a speeding train for the notorious rebel: he found it difficult to abandon after it had once got started. The Sutton-Taylor feud came to a head when Jack Helm made a personal visit to Hardin. He praised him as the fastest draw in Texas, and argued that if Hardin joined his faction, the Taylors would be eliminated and peace would finally return to Gonzalez County. Hardin refused; since becoming a father, he was merely a neutral observer to the conflict. The feud did not allow for neutral observers, however. The next day, Hardin returned home to find his wife terrified and weeping. Helm and 50 followers had been there demanding to know where Hardin was so that they could end his miserable life. Hardin did not wait for them to come and bully his wife again. He looked up Jim Taylor immediately, and rode out with a number of men. They did not return home until they had planted bullets in the heads of both Jack Helm and his partner, Bill Sutton.

The murder of Bill Sutton on the deck of a boat in broad daylight outraged Texans, from Governor Richard Coke right down to the simplest dirt farmer. They had all believed that the installation of the new governor in November 1873 spelled the end of factional violence in Texas. Immediately, the Texas Rangers were reinstated and vested with the authority to put an end to the ruffians who evidently hated peace. John Wesley Hardin was on the top of their list.

Hardin, meanwhile, had moved his young family away from explosive Gonzalez County to Comanche in central Texas. He was vaguely aware that all the killing was not providing the best example for his child.

On his 21st birthday, May 26, 1874, he was celebrating in the local saloon. On that very day, a Texas Ranger named Charles Webb rode into town to capture or kill the birthday boy.

Not knowing that Hardin may have been forewarned, Webb headed for the local saloon. As he was about to enter, a wiry young man stepped in front of him and blocked his path.

The young man spread his coat back to reveal two pistols. "Do you have papers for my arrest?" he asked Webb haughtily.

"I don't know who you are," lied Webb, suddenly conscious of the heat and the people gathering around them. Perspiration beaded his forehead.

"My name is John Wesley Hardin, and I understand you're here to arrest me." The gray eyes of the young man peered narrowly at the Ranger.

Webb hesitated. His target stood before him, brazen and fearless. He replied, "Now I know who you are, but I don't have any papers for your arrest."

"Then come and have a drink with me, it's my birthday," said Hardin amicably. The stranger's answer seemed to have satisfied him. He turned to enter the coolness of the saloon. Suddenly someone screamed out a warning. Hardin whirled and cross-drew in one fluid motion, his guns blazing. Webb had been the first to draw but was the first to fall. Hardin's bullet rocketed into the forehead of the deputy, whose single shot nevertheless caught Hardin in the side. Mortally wounded, Webb fell to the ground. As he did so, his gun went off again, sending its futile bullet ripping into the side of the building. Hardin's friends, Jim Taylor and Bud Dixon, then walked up to the deputy sheriff and pumped his body full of lead.

The witnesses to the killing were appalled. Had the war destroyed all memory of peace? John Wesley Hardin was a dangerous force beyond all control. A lynch mob formed like lightning, and for the first time in his life, Hardin felt the scorching heat of unanimous hate beating down upon him. Confused, he leapt to his horse and rode hard out of town.

The times, and Texas, had changed.

Hardin's relatives suffered in his place. An enraged mob led by crazed and bloodthirsty Texas Rangers seized Hardin's peaceful brother Joe and four cousins, and dragged them outside of town. A couple of tall trees served for the lynching.

Using the name J.H. Swain, Hardin moved his family to Florida. The Texas government promptly posted a reward of $4000 for the capture of the outlaw, dead or alive.

Hardin murdered two detectives who came after him, and moved his family again, this time to Alabama. Jane gave birth to a son, and then another daughter, and it looked as if trouble was slipping into the past.

But the Texas Rangers were determined that Hardin be brought to justice, regardless of whether it was the judiciary's or God's. They assigned John Armstrong to head up the officers who would hunt Hardin down and avenge the death of Webb. Armstrong recognized that force would not necessarily prevail in bringing the famous outlaw to the ground. He thus opted for a more circuitous method. He cultivated a friendship with a cowboy who was boarding at the Hardin homestead in Texas, and told him to pass on any news of the relatives who were not at home. The desired information was not long in coming. Jane, homesick for her kin back home, wrote to them from Alabama with news of her newfound peacefulness. The Rangers pounced.

In August 1877, Armstrong and his men arrived in Alabama, armed, wary and determined not to come up empty-handed. They learned that Hardin was traveling by train from a gambling junket in Florida with an associate named Jim Mann. The two dozen heavily armed Rangers headed to Pensacola and boarded the train there.

As the train rolled through the still, hot night of August 23, Hardin dozed. His hand cradled his head. His elbow was propped on the open window. The air was muggy, and Hardin slumped uncomfortably in his seat. Mann was across from him, listless and sluggish. Neither of them took notice of the movement at the end of the coach, where a number of new arrivals had entered.

Armstrong had deployed his Rangers throughout the train and then took a seat diagonally across from Hardin. Armstrong studied the outlaw's face in the gathering dusk to make sure that he had the right man. Nodding, the big man stood up, planted his feet firmly apart, cocked his pistol and placed it against Hardin's temple. "Don't move, Mr. Hardin, and I won't be forced to kill you," he drawled. Hardin turned slightly, forced a weak smile, and then like lightning convulsed in a motion that combined the reaching for the pistols with the ducking of his head. For the first time, Hardin's quick draw failed: the trigger guard of his pistol snagged on his suspenders and caught him in a tangle. The delay was not lost on Armstrong, who brought down his own gun with vicious weight on the outlaw's head. The blow knocked Hardin out of his seat. Jim Mann leveled his pistol and ripped off a shot that tore through the Ranger's hat. The bullet whistled harmlessly past Armstrong's scalp. Acrid gun smoke confused the scene. Armstrong whirled and fired at close range. His shot was a direct hit. Wounded, Mann jumped from the train, but was dead within minutes. Hardin lay unconscious on the coach floor, which was now slick with blood.

Texas's most wanted killer had been captured alive.

John Wesley Hardin went on trial in Gonzales, Texas, for the murder of Charles Webb. He was sentenced to 25 years in jail for second-degree murder. He was defiant at first, but the jailers soon broke him. Thereafter, he became a model prisoner and used the prison library to study law.

His wife remained steadfastly faithful to him, but died before his release.

He was set free in 1894 on a pardon from the governor. He moved to El Paso and wrote his autobiography.

Eventually, his temper flared up again. He fell into former ways and picked a fight with a family named Selman.

On July 19, 1895, Hardin was leaning against the bar in the Acme Saloon playing dice and drinking whiskey. When it came his turn to roll, he threw the dice up in the air, and then watched them hop and skitter. When they finally came to rest, he squinted at the numbers shown, and then exulted, "Four sixes!" Then he looked up. In the big mirror behind the

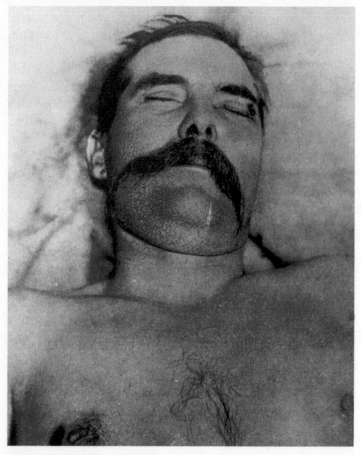

JOHN WESLEY HARDIN IN DEATH

bar, his image blurred by smoke, was an old man. Did Hardin see the reflection of John Selman Sr., a rifle raised to his eye? Or was he blinded by some last vision of himself, a worn-out gunman whose glory was past? For whatever reason, the fastest draw in Texas did not turn. A second later, John Wesley Hardin was dead, with a bullet in his brain.

The violent product of the Civil War and the enemy of Reconstruction was dead. Reconstruction itself had failed in the last of the southern states in 1877. The Civil War had succeeded in the official abolition of slavery, but with the rejection of Republican governments and the formation of the "solid South," old enmities entrenched themselves again. Racism thrived with a vengeance, and many of its political and social effects would be felt long into the next century. The Civil War stamped a generation, and marked men like John Wesley Hardin with an unstoppable violence. Famous individuals live on in the public imagination, but the legacy of war is another matter: the preacher's son who took to his guns is born again, every time slow-moving words are abandoned for faster weapons.

MARY AND JESSE JR., THE CHILDREN OF JESSE JAMES

5

Jesse James

Frank reined in his horse and wildly fired at the advancing citizens. Jesse rolled and jumped up. As the bullets flew, he charged toward his waiting brother.

Missouri has raised some remarkable citizens for the United States—Mark Twain and President Harry S. Truman spring to mind—but the Missourian who has done most to shape American identity was neither a great writer nor a prominent statesman, but a man who, in a time of shifting uncertainty, stuck to the one thing he knew he could trust.

Many a change had swept through the State of Missouri by the time Jesse James strode onto the stage. Situated on the border of East and West, and North and South, Missouri was admitted to the United States in 1821. By then St. Louis was already a city of respectable size, and the state was well-known as a jumping-off point for pioneers, Indian agents and adventurers heading north and west. Missouri had been admitted to the Union as a slave state, but the state was split on the issue of slavery. Aggressive settlement of nearby

Kansas by Northern abolitionists in the 1850s provoked Missourians, for although only a few owned slaves, most hailed from slave-owning families. Extremists were already at war on the Missouri-Kansas border when the Civil War broke out in 1861. Missouri attempted to appease both sides, and sided with itself: a state convention found no reason to join the secessionist South, but also chose a position of armed neutrality to resist invasion by Union soldiers. Second perhaps only to Virginia, Missouri suffered the worst fighting. Even after Union forces routed the Confederates at Pea Ridge in 1862, guerrillas such as William Quantrill and "Bloody Bill" Anderson remained active throughout the Missourian countryside. Nor did the violence cease in April 1865 when the Civil War ended.

The story of the action-hungry, murderous bandit who terrorized banks and railroads, fascinated newspapermen from New York to Kansas City and set the tone of Missouri politics for a score of years has as much to do with these turbulent times as it does with the ideals of a family and home.

Newspaperman John Newman Edwards gave us the Jesse James we know today. It was he who first fit Jesse to the mold of Robin Hood. He was the first to present Jesse as the lawbreaking hero who robbed in the fairness of broad daylight. In his editorial "The Chivalry of Crime" for the Kansas City *Times* on September 28, 1872, Edwards praised the daringness of the crime (Jesse had just robbed the Kansas City Fair), while at the same time denying the guilt of the criminal. He likened Jesse James to King Arthur and Ivanhoe. With this comparison, he recreated the contradiction—albeit an alluring one—of the bloody idealist.

And the contradiction has persisted, for never has there been an outlaw as loved and hated as Jesse James.

Jesse Woodson James was born on September 5, 1847. His parents were Robert James, a Baptist minister, and Zerelda Cole James. Not much is known about his childhood except that he was preceded into the world by his brother Frank. In 1850, when young Jesse was three, his father went west in search of gold. He never returned. Cholera claimed his life shortly after his arrival in California.

Zerelda remarried and then quickly separated from her second husband. Her third husband, whom she married in 1855, was Reuben Samuel, a doctor and a farmer. Jesse was eight years old before he met his stepfather. Samuel was by all accounts a good man, and he and Zerelda had four children—Archie, John, Sallie and Fannie.

The home where Frank and Jesse James grew up was in Clay County, Missouri, which lies on the north side of the Missouri River not far from Kansas City. The main towns in Clay County were Liberty, where Frank and Jesse arguably robbed their first bank, Kearney, where Jesse was baptized after the Civil War, and Missouri City. Jackson County and the town of Independence lie to the south of Clay, and St. Joseph, where Jesse spent the last years of his life, a little to the north. Robert and Zerelda had come from Kentucky and settled in Clay County in 1842, and neither of Zerelda's subsequent marriages took her away from it.

Legend has it that Jesse James began his violent career as a free-wheeling gunslinger because of his family.

At the start of the Civil War, the 18-year-old Frank James joined the Home Guards of Clay County, who vowed to defend their homes and families from outside attack. They were not secessionists at first, but they also refused to do the dirty work of the bluecoats. The bluecoats, for their part, insisted the dirty work be done. Wave after wave of General Henry W. Halleck's Union soldiers flooded into Missouri and beat back the Confederate forces under Governor Jackson and his general, Sterling Price. By early 1862, the Confederate Army had been forced to retreat into Arkansas.

It was then the guerrilla war began.

Frustrated at defeat and intent on return, General Price sent secret recruiting agents back into Missouri to muster support. The agents' method was not exactly one of mild persuasion. They directly convinced only 5000 men to rally behind Price, but destroyed as much of Missouri's infrastructure—from bridges and trains to telegraph wires—as they could on their sweep through the state. General Halleck ordered the on-site shooting of the perpetrators of this destruction, and clamped down on the citizenry. When innocent civilians began to be abused by suspicious Union soldiers, their young men swore allegiance to the South, and "went to the brush."

Frank James was one of these men. He rode under the black flag of William Quantrill, crossing paths with Cole Younger, Joseph Shelby and Shelby's adjutant, John Newman Edwards, who would play such an important journalistic role later. Quantrill's bloodiest raid was in Lawrence, Kansas, on August 21, 1863. The raid came in retaliation for the Union's attempt to control the families of known guerrillas. Wives, mothers and sisters of Quantrill's men, including the sister of "Bloody Bill" Anderson, had been killed, and the irregulars fought back with the rage of rabid dogs. They chose Lawrence because of old resentment from the days before the war, in which Lawrence had established itself as a Northern stronghold. Quantrill and his men slaughtered 150 men and boys on that day, and the women were forced to watch.

The oldtimers of Clay County say that the Union soldiers came to the Samuel farm shortly thereafter. They were looking for Frank. A fiery Zerelda Samuel told them to ask the women of Lawrence, for she herself hadn't seen him lately. Incensed, the soldiers tortured Reuben Samuel, and hurled insults at the pregnant Zerelda. Then they advanced on the 16-year-old brother of the known guerrilla. Jesse ran from them through the soft soil of the fields that night, but the soldiers caught him, questioned him and whipped him until they could whip no more.

At last, the dark shapes folded up their whips and left. Jesse lay where he had been lashed. When he had sufficiently recovered, he stood up. The path he now would walk was clear. He looked up, saw the bright window of his mother's home, and began, painfully, to trudge towards it.

A short time later, he joined the guerrillas.

William Quantrill had been superseded by "Bloody Bill" Anderson when Jesse joined his brother Frank in 1864. Anderson was impressed with Jesse, and said that he was a good fighter for a man without a beard. In August 1864, Jesse took a bullet in the right side of his chest during a battle, but lived on. He proved his mettle a month later during a raid that history would refer to as the Centralia Massacre.

On September 27, 1864, Anderson led 30 of his men into the little town of Centralia near Columbia, Missouri. The exact reason for the raid on this particular town is unclear; war loses track of reasons. Anderson's men hollered and plundered all morning, and when the stagecoach from Columbia arrived, its passengers were greeted by the sight of a burning railroad depot and the order to hand over their possessions. At noon, a train carrying two dozen unarmed soldiers of the Union rolled in, and the matter took a turn for the worse. Anderson's men ripped open the door, and drove the cowering passengers from the cars. A legacy of crime was born in that moment, when the eyes of Jesse James beheld a train being overpowered and gutted by ruthless men brandishing their guns in the faces of their fellow human beings.

The defenseless soldiers were stripped of their uniforms, shoved into line and brutally massacred.

After the slaughter, Anderson's men took to their horses, and galloped away from the column of smoke that announced the consequences of their raid far and wide. They were soon pursued by Union soldiers under the command of Major A.V.E. Johnson. Johnson's cavalry caught up to Anderson and his band of irregulars, who, when they saw that they could not outrun their pursuers, whirled around to fight. Johnson and his men leapt from their horses to brace for the attack. Dismounting was a fatal error. The mounted guerrillas slashed through the bluecoats like scythes through grass. Soldier after federal soldier was ridden down, shot or stabbed; only a handful escaped death that day. And when the destruction finally ceased, the cutdown bodies of the bluecoats littered the field, and Jesse James was lifted up by his fellows, for it was determined that his bullet had killed Major Johnson.

When the Civil War ended, Missouri entered a new period of turmoil. Republicans and Democrats jockeyed for position as the countryside awoke from the horror of the guerrilla war and began ever so slowly to rebuild. People were thrown back on their own resources during the rise up out of the shambles. For most of them, family was the only reliable support. It is no surprise, then, that the most notorious partners in Reconstruction Missouri were also brothers.

Those who fought for the South had their rights revoked when the Radical Republicans took over at the end of the war. Ex-Confederates were not officially pardoned for crimes committed during wartime by the new state constitution of 1865, but most were treated leniently by the Radicals and were allowed to surrender without additional punishment. Frank James was one of them. Jesse James was not.

According to legend, Jesse James tried to surrender in the summer of 1865, but as he was riding toward Lexington under a white flag, Union soldiers opened fire on him. Again, he was wounded in the right side of the chest, but escaped. Alone in the wilderness, he lay himself down in the cold waters of a creek to keep his fever at bay that night, and a farmer found him the following morning. The farmer helped him to friends, who in turn sent Jesse to his family. In Kansas City, Jesse's cousin, Zee Mimms, tenderly nursed him back to health. Before leaving Zee, Jesse promised to marry her.

Then he and Frank began their new career. A bank in Liberty, Missouri had the dubious honor of being the first to fall prey to Frank and Jesse James.

February 13, 1866 was a dark day. When the pale sun had passed its zenith and began once more to slip toward the horizon, a dozen horsemen rode into the town of Liberty, and stoically took up positions along the street. Two of them were muffled up in blue coats of the Union. The two men tied up their mounts and entered the Clay County Savings Bank. One lingered by the stove, while the other walked up to cashier William Bird to ask for change. A bared pistol suddenly changed the nature and amount of the transaction. The bandit leapt across the counter, struck the cashier on the head and ordered him into the safe. A sack was thrust into Bird's hands and he was forced to stuff it with as much money as it would hold. By this time, the other bandit had also slid across the counter. He ordered the other cashier, who happened to be William's father, into the safe as well. The robbers then swung the door shut in order to imprison their victims, and dashed out of the bank with $60,000 of Union money in their grasp.

No one would have realized that the bank had just been robbed, had not one of the robbers begun to shoot. An innocent bystander named George Wymore was killed. The bandits then charged south out of town. They forced the ferryman to take them across the cold and sluggish river. The weather cooperated with their dark designs: the fury of a hissing snowstorm obliterated all evidence of their escape. A posse of citizens and lawmen was forced to abandon pursuit and concede that the outlaws had vanished.

Similar robberies followed at Lexington, Savannah and Richmond. The crime wave spilled out of Missouri when the bandits hit the bank in Russelville, Kentucky. But it was not until the robbery in Gallatin that the names of the James brothers were connected to their crimes.

On December 7, 1869, John W. Sheets was attending to business as usual in the Daviess County Savings Bank in Gallatin, Missouri, a town about 70 miles northeast of Kansas City. His assistant, William A. McDowell, was also present when a stranger walked in and asked for change for a $100 bill. Sheets complied, and opened the safe. Before he could count out the money another man entered the bank. Apparently, he had overheard the first man's request.

He announced that he had the change required and would take it in exchange for the $100 bill.

Undisturbed by the coincidence that the second man had exactly the change that the first man wanted, Sheets sat down to fill out the necessary paperwork. The second man continued on toward the counter. In a single, fluid motion, and without breaking his stride, the second man pulled out his revolver and fired. The bullet shot through John W. Sheet's brain and killed him instantly. Before he could slide to the ground, a second bullet from the same gun had sliced through his heart.

William McDowell bolted like a deer. The bandits whirled and shot at him, and McDowell took a bullet in the arm but kept running. He burst out onto the wintry street.

"Murder!" he screamed. "Captain Sheets has been murdered!"

His cry ripped through the sleepy town like lightning.

Some passers-by jumped for cover; other citizens scrambled for their guns and converged on the bank. Having had the safe opened for them, the robbers were soon out on the street with a suspiciously swollen sack. The first thief made it up onto his horse, but just as the second thief was about to swing astride his animal, a flurry of gunfire scared it into a trot. The rider's foot got caught in the stirrup; he was dragged 30 feet down the frosty road before finally kicking free of the tangle of legs and leather.

That could have been the end of Jesse James, right there on the stone-cold streets of Gallatin, had not his partner also been his blood relation. Frank reined in his horse and wildly fired at the advancing citizens. Jesse rolled and jumped up. As the bullets flew, he charged towards his waiting brother. He sprang up behind Frank, who fired one last shot in warning before turning toward the open country. Bearing both brothers, the steadfast horse galloped out of town. A hurriedly organized posse soon set out after the bandits.

The brothers, meanwhile, had stolen another horse at the first available opportunity, and they forced a farmer to guide them through the countryside until they reached the tracks of the railroad. Once there, they were home free, for as the chase continued, the landscape became less and less familiar to the posse and more and more familiar to the prey. Nevertheless, it became clear that the bandits were angling toward Clay County.

And nothing they could do could eliminate the 700-pound piece of evidence they had left behind. The townsmen quickly secured Jesse's horse and began searching for its owner. The local paper warned that the bandits had been thoroughly described and immediately identified, and that they would not escape capture.

The search did not take long. A few days after the robbery in Gallatin, two men from that town joined forces with Deputy Sheriff John S. Thomason from Liberty, and rode out to the Samuel farm. It was common knowledge in Clay County that the horse in the lawmen's possession belonged to Jesse James. Thomason's son Oscar accompanied the party. Upon arrival, two of the men hid in the forest within sight of the back of the house. The sheriff and his son approached the house from the front.

No one came out to greet them.

They got off their horses, and began to walk toward the front door. The law, after all, was on their side, but the quiet motionlessness of the farmyard unnerved them. Who would be waiting behind the door?

Suddenly something moved, off to their left. Thomason started and reached for his pistol. The commotion was a small black boy who took no notice of the lawmen and ran past them towards the stable.

Still, it only takes a small spark to light a stick of dynamite. Thomason walked on toward the front door, but Oscar paused and watched the boy run. When the boy reached the stable, he disappeared, and for a moment all was still.

With the force of an explosion, the door to the stable burst open, and Frank and Jesse James shot out from the darkness. Their guns blazed, and their bodies were bent low over their horses. Thomason squeezed off a few harmless shots before diving for cover. Oscar also took aim, but, in the surprise of the moment, failed to hit the felons. The bandits veered off into the field beside the house and sped like bullets toward the fence. They barreled straight at it, sprang, and sailed into the open country beyond.

The Gallatin men came pounding out of the woods, but their horses shied away from the daring leap. Oscar's horse also refused to make the jump, and turned so sharply at the fence that he was almost thrown from the saddle. Only his father's horse cleared the fence. The elder Thomason raced on alone after the fleeing outlaws, but when he took aim and shot, his horse bucked and he crashed to the ground. He rose in time to see the bandits vanish into the distance.

The James brothers had escaped capture, but they had not escaped notice. The next day, both the Kansas City *Times* and the Liberty *Tribune* connected their names to the robbery in Gallatin. Governor Joseph W. McClurg tried to organize a manhunt, but his efforts failed. One reason for the failure was that the James brothers knew the country like the back of their hands. Another reason was that Clay County was not at all convinced that the James boys had done anything wrong. Frank and Jesse undoubtedly found refuge in countless farmhouses, where loyalty to family was respected over loyalty to the Union.

A few days after the daring race from the Samuel farm, John Newman Edwards published the first of the many letters allegedly written by Jesse James in defense of his innocence. The Kansas City *Times* carried the piece. In it, Jesse stated that he had not killed Captain Sheets. He had not been anywhere near Gallatin on December 7, and had alibis to prove it. Furthermore, he refused to turn himself in to certain death at the hands of his enemies from the Civil War: "I never will surrender to be mobbed by a set of bloodthirsty poltroons."

Needless to say, Jesse James remained at large.

No one knows exactly how the James brothers decided which banks to rob. Their choice might have been random. But the choice to rob banks, specifically, as opposed to stores or travelers, was not random. Because so many banks were set up after the war during the reorganization of the Southern economy, the banks became a hated symbol of Northern domination. The James brothers were not alone in raiding banks in Reconstruction Missouri out of a sense of resentment, but over the course of time the actions of many were telescoped into the actions of a few.

On June 3, 1871, Cole Younger and Clell Miller helped Jesse James and his brother Frank rob the bank in Corydon, Iowa. Miller was a young man from Kearney, and Younger an old associate of Frank's from William Quantrill's band of guerrillas. Their timing was impeccable; their crime took place while most of the town was at the Methodist Church, listening to Henry Clay Dean speak in favor of putting a railroad through Corydon. The bandits easily overpowered the lone clerk at the bank, and bound him hand and foot. They sauntered out the door with $6000 tucked away into their pockets. Before leaving town, one of the band members barged into the Church and announced what had just happened.

"The bank has been robbed!" he yelled.

The citizens turned, and stared him down. "Shush!" someone called. "For shame!" admonished another. "How dare you interrupt Mr. Dean!" called a third. The bandit shrugged, turned around and left. He joined his fellows, and they trotted out of town. Half an hour elapsed before the townspeople realized that the stranger had not been calling wolf.

In April 1872, the James-Younger Gang hit the bank in Columbia, Kentucky, where they shot the cashier dead and lifted $600. At the Kansas City Fair five months later, Jesse struck again.

The cashier at the gate of the fair had his feet up after a hectic morning, when a man with sandy-colored whiskers walked up to the booth and gestured at the cashbox.

"What if I was to say I was Jesse James," asked the man, "and told you to hand out that tin box of money—what would you say?"

The cashier picked at his teeth a moment before answering.

"Well," he drawled, considering, "I'd say I'd see you in hell first."

The man casually pulled out a pistol and replied, "Well, that's just who I am—Jesse James—and you had better hand it out pretty damned quick, or else." The cashier started to his feet, but froze when he saw the aggressor's eyes narrow in determination. Close to $1000 was stolen, and in the press the next day, John Newman Edwards glorified the boldness of the bandit.

Frank and Jesse James were now the most notorious outlaws of their time in the United States. With the Younger brothers—Cole, Jim, John and Bob—the James brothers robbed banks with such mercilessness and bravado that their crimes were discussed as far away as Chicago, New York and Washington. Each crime was followed by sensational reactions in the press. Soon a pattern established itself. After a crime, the James boys were publicly defended by their mother, who proclaimed her boys' innocence and denounced their treacherous accusers. Through John Newman Edward's influence, letters allegedly written by Jesse James continued to appear in the newspapers. Pursuing lawmen met with little, if any, success after the crimes. The victims were not much help. The names of Frank and Jesse James were about as well known as apple pie in the 1870s, and yet their faces were somehow singularly forgettable. Hardly any witnesses stepped forward to offer testimony, and if they did, they often mysteriously changed their mind before helping. A woman named Mattie Hamlet was one of these. She proudly crowed that she had seen the notorious Jesse James rob a stagecoach at Lexington, until she received a visit from Zerelda Samuel advising her not to draw attention to herself in such an unladylike fashion.

At Council Bluffs, Iowa, the legacy of the Centralia Massacre was fulfilled. It was here that the James-Younger Gang robbed its first train. Late at night on July 21, 1873, the bandits pulled one of the rails of the Chicago, Rock Island and Pacific Railroad out of position, just as a train was rounding the corner. Engineer John Rafferty saw what was happening and yanked on the brakes. The train screeched to a halt. Rafferty had saved all the lives on board but his own; only the engine toppled from the rails, but its fall killed the engineer within. Spectral shapes swarmed the train. The bandits had disguised themselves in the white hoods and cloaks of the Klu Klux Klan. They stole $2000 from the express safe before melting away into the darkness of the woods.

Outrage over the death of John Rafferty did little to hamper the outlaws. They brought their train-robbing tactics home to Missouri when they struck at Gads Hill on January 31, 1874.

Jesse James had by this time emerged as the undisputed leader of the band. On April 24, 1874, he crowned his achievements with a wedding. Zee and Jesse were married by a Methodist preacher in Kansas City, and the news was giddily broken by a St. Louis newspaper within two months. As the domestic bliss of Jesse James peaked, so too did the danger in which he lived.

The Pinkerton National Detective Agency had taken an interest in the James-Younger Gang ever since the robbery at Corydon, and after the train heist at Gads Hill, it began to pursue the James brothers in earnest. The detectives were employed by the railroads, which could afford to pay the expert Pinkerton men. Penetrating rural Missouri to bring down the James boys was a daunting task, and the Pinkerton detectives should have better analyzed the case and their role in it before making their move.

Detective John W. Whicher showed up in Liberty on March 10, 1874, talking about capturing the wanted outlaws at their home on the Samuel farm. He confided in the president of the bank, D.J. Adkins, and the former sheriff, O.P. Moss. Adkins and Moss tried to dissuade Whicher from his foolish plan of hiring on at the Samuel farm and surprising Frank and Jesse with betrayal. Clay County was not the sort of place where strangers were immediately trusted—especially strangers with traces of a Yankee accent in their speech. Whicher stubbornly stuck to his plan and set out for the Samuel farm in a thin disguise.

His murdered body was found the following morning in a ditch on the south side of the Missouri River, not far from Independence. The corpse had bullet holes in the chest and the head. The attempt by a Northerner backed by Northern corporations to infiltrate a good, old-fashioned Southern family met with disaster, and there were many in Clay County who hotly avowed that Whicher had got what he deserved.

The foolhardy move by the Pinkertons only incited Frank and Jesse James to bolder exploits. On December 7 and 8, 1874, the James-Younger Gang pulled off the dual robbery of the Tishimingo Bank in Corinth, Mississippi, and the Kansas Pacific Railroad at Muncie, Kansas. The two crimes occurred over 500 miles distant from each other, and yet only a few hours elapsed between the two. The press, usually quick to attribute such ambitious crimes to the James-Younger Gang, was at a loss to explain the impossible timing. For a while, it looked as though supporters of the James brothers had been right all along: Frank and Jesse were accused of crimes they did not commit—and could not possibly have committed, given their concurrence. Gradually, however, another explanation surfaced. The James-Younger Gang had grown into a cunning company of well-organized criminals who could orchestrate a two-pronged, simultaneous attack.

The Pinkertons struck again on the night of January 26, 1875. Two other agents had fallen in the line of duty since Whicher's death, and their next move appeared to be one of deadly vengeance.

Reuben and Zerelda Samuel woke with a start when an object crashed through the window of their farmhouse and landed in their kitchen. They dashed into the kitchen to find it lit by diabolic flames: the object, wrapped in fuel-soaked cotton, was on fire. Reuben grabbed a shovel and whisked the fireball into the fireplace, where it could burn itself out without threatening the building. By this time, the children had awoken and ventured into the room. Nine-year-old Archie was in front. The Samuels hardly had time to breathe a sigh of relief when a second burning missile crashed suddenly into their midst.

"Stay back!" shouted Reuben, as he scooped it up and shoveled it into the fireplace. Unlike its predecessor, the second fireball exploded when it hit the grate. A jagged part of it slashed into Zerelda's hand, but the largest fragment shot across the room and, with the force of a cannon blast, ripped into Archie's side.

Zerelda screamed.

Archie slid to the ground, his life slipping away. He did not cry; his eyes flickered with the searing pain.

"Mother," he said. "Mommy." He died within the hour.

When daylight finally stole upon the sleepless household, Reuben combed the yard for clues left by the attackers. Though blinded by tears, he stumbled across a pistol that someone had dropped in the night. He picked it up, brushed it off and saw that inscribed in it were the letters "P.G.G."

The letters were the abbreviation for "Pinkerton Government Guard."

The backlash against the assault on the Samuel home could not have been harsher. Once they realized that they could not escape the blame, the detectives admitted to committing the raid. They disavowed all intent to injure, and explained that the objects had been illumination devices, which should have been harmless. They hadn't wanted to hurt anyone: if Reuben had left the device alone, the coals from the hearth would not have caused it to explode. The detectives' explanation fell on deaf ears. Young Archie was dead, and Zerelda's right hand had to be amputated. The Missouri press raged against the cowardice of federal agents who would choose to attack a sleeping family. Popular opinion agreed that no amount of thievery could justify the bombing of a family home by government officials. Even the state government joined the roar of outrage against the detectives. A resolution to launch an inquiry into the incident was passed overwhelmingly by the House of Representatives, and also by the Senate. (The resolution ultimately led the House to a long debate and crucial vote on whether or not the James brothers should be granted amnesty by the state legislature.) No one could excuse the lawmen for killing a little boy.

No one, least of all Jesse James.

On April 12, 1875, Daniel Askew, a neighbor of the Samuels', was found murdered on his doorstep. He had been suspected of helping the Pinkerton detectives on the night of their attack.

On September 5, 1875, $10,000 was stolen from a bank in Huntington, West Virginia. Despite the distance from Missouri, the James-Younger Gang was suspected, for one of its members was shot down and another captured.

On July 7, 1876, a train of the Missouri Pacific Railroad was stopped and looted at Rocky Cut, near Otterville, Missouri. The singing of religious songs by the passengers during the heist did not deter the determined thieves.

The last attack by the James-Younger Gang occurred September 7, 1876 at the First National Bank in Northfield, Minnesota, 400 miles north of Clay County.

Six men rode with Frank and Jesse James that day. Clell Miller, the accomplice at Corydon, was there, as were William Stiles and Samuel Wells. Cole Younger and his brothers Bob and Jim made up the other three. (The last Younger, John, had been killed by Pinkerton agents in a shoot-out in 1874.) Following their usual pattern, the gang members took up various positions upon entering the town. Some lingered on the outskirts, two stationed themselves on the main street and the last three dismounted and walked into the bank.

"Open the safe," barked the leader, without breaking his stride. Jesse James was not one to waste time.

The cashier, whose name was Joseph L. Heywood, courageously refused to obey. He died for his disobedience: unwilling to argue, one of the bandits leapt across the counter, drew his knife and slit Heywood's throat. As the innocent man crumpled to the ground, the bandit pumped him full of lead to vent his frustration.

Teller A.E. Bunker bolted like a deer.

He took a bullet in the shoulder blade, but managed to stumble out onto the street to raise the alarm. The two guards were already having trouble keeping the street clear of people, and when the teller emerged shouting, "Murder!" they began firing. A Swedish man named Nicholas Gustavson was caught in the confusion. He was unable to understand the bandits' frenzied warning and was gunned down for his hesitation.

The citizens of Northfield reacted with remarkable speed. Within moments they had seized weapons and arrayed themselves in a line of defense across from the bank. Gunfire crackled as the three bandits who had been posted on the edge of town raced to the aid of their fellows. Clell Miller took a bullet in the chest and pitched forward into the dust of the street, dead. One of the bandits' horses was also shot down. By this time, the three main robbers had abandoned their attempt to open the safe. They burst from the bank with blazing pistols, and scrambled for their horses. William Stiles stood up to cover them, but he was kicked off his feet by a close-range shotgun blast. His body fell in the open and twitched under the rain of angry bullets. Bob Younger was also hit, but Frank and Jesse James made their horses, and, in the company of the remaining outlaws, spurred them away from the scene of carnage. Cole whirled his horse back into the fray when he realized that Bob was missing. His crazed charge threw the citizens off their advantage, and in the brief moments it took them to regroup, he grabbed his younger brother by the scruff of the neck and hauled him up onto the back of his horse. His feet dangling uselessly above the ground, Bob Younger was carried out of Northfield alive.

The outlaws escaped, but the lawmen ensured that they would not get far. The sympathetic population of Clay County was a long way off, and dozens of law-abiding communities stood between the outlaws and their place of refuge. A massive manhunt took form as the sheriffs and deputies passed the descriptions of the bandits on to their colleagues.

The bandits, meanwhile, staggered south. Jesse rode at the front, scouting the lay of the land, and turning around periodically to urge greater speed. He was nervous; none of them really had any idea where they were. The sight of the wounded, pathetic Bob weighing down his brother filled Jesse James with an indescribable foreboding.

He soon slackened his pace. As the others trotted up to him, he turned his horse to face Cole Younger squarely.

"Let him down," he said to Cole, gesturing at the weak and wounded man.

Cole dismounted and eased Bob onto the ground. Bob squinted with pain and his breathing was shallow. Cole propped him up with his saddlebag. Jesse waited until Bob was comfortable before speaking again.

"Kill him," he said.

Cole Younger gazed at Jesse, aghast.

"Kill him," Jesse repeated, nodding at the man wounded on the ground.

"What?" whispered the eldest Younger. Disbelief stung his face.

"That man is getting in our way. He ain't doing nothing except slowing us down, and what's more, he's leaving a blood trail 'bout as plain as day." Jesse stared at Cole as he spoke. He was numb now to the words that issued from his lips, numb to the scathing betrayal mirrored back at him by the injury on his men's faces. No one dared move. Jesse pointed once again at Bob. "It's him or us."

Bitter desolation seeped into Cole's eyes. Weakness and fear trembled on his lip. And then all signs of emotion were quenched by an implacable emptiness.

"Go to hell, Jesse James," he breathed.

Samuel Wells still had some spunk in him when the manhunt netted him. He shot at the approaching lawmen and was gunned down. The posse soon found the Younger brothers, starving and half-frozen. Cole, Jim and Bob thought they would be lynched right there and then, but the Minnesotans surprised them. The lawmen took them to the nearest town, fed them and got them warm. Then they transported their captives to the jail at Faribault.

The Younger brothers stood trial for the murder and attempted robbery at Northfield. They pleaded guilty to the crime. Under Minnesota law, the stiffest penalty that could be imposed on a defendant who pleaded guilty was life imprisonment. Accordingly, they were sentenced and served their term at the Minnesota penitentiary in Stillwater.

Frank and Jesse James split off from the others during their flight from Northfield, and escaped the posses. They won some respite from their pursuers after crossing the state boundary line into Iowa, and they pressed on eagerly for the familiar counties of Missouri.

Missouri, however, had heard the news from Northfield. Missouri had heard of the cold-blooded murder of a brave cashier and of the bewildering murder of an innocent foreigner. Missouri had seen pictures of the Youngers, shackled and imprisoned, captured easily by a state that had a clear reputation for law and order. It was obvious who the two men were who had gotten away. Not one in 10 staunch ex-Confederates would defend the James brothers now.

Jesse and Frank assumed different names and fled with their families to Tennessee. For three years after Northfield, not a peep was heard from them. But then, on October 8, 1879, a train was robbed at Glendale, near Independence, Missouri. Another train robbery followed at Winston, near Kansas City, on July 15, 1881, and during this robbery, the bandits killed a passenger named Frank McMillan. A third train fell prey to robbery at Blue Cut, quite close to Glendale, on September 7, 1881, and the new governor, Thomas T. Crittenden, decided that the notorious Jesse James finally had to be stopped once and for all. A reward of $10,000 from Crittenden's own pocket—or, at least, the pocket of his financiers—was offered in exchange for the body of Jesse James, dead or alive.

On April 3, 1882, Bob Ford laid claim to that money.

Jesse had moved his family back up to Missouri after their time in Tennessee. Although he was the most notorious outlaw of his day, almost no one knew his face, and he and his family walked through the streets of Kansas City and St. Joseph, where they made their new home, without any fear of recognition. It was at his home in St. Joseph that Jesse was finally laid low. But no badged lawman earned the honor

ROBERT FORD

THE HOME OF JESSE AND ZEE JAMES, ST. JOSEPH, MISSOURI

of catching the famous bandit. Jesse James was betrayed by one of his own.

He had just risen from the breakfast table, which he had shared that April morning with Charles and Bob Ford, two new members of his gang. He went into the main room, and

dropped his guns on a bed before climbing onto a chair to dust and adjust a painting. When his back was turned, Bob Ford drew his pistol and, covered by his brother, shot Jesse in the back of the head. He died instantly. His wife ran into the room, threw herself on his body and wept bitterly. When the authorities arrived, she tried at first to pretend that the dead man's name was Howard, but then broke down and admitted that it was her Jesse.

As soon as he had fired the fatal shot, Bob Ford ran out of the house to announce his feat to Governor Crittenden, and claim his reward. Jesse did not know Bob Ford all that well, but Charles had taken part in the robbery at Blue Cut. Jesse had admitted Bob to the gang, and trusted him, because he was Charles's brother.

Shortly after the betrayal and assassination of his brother, Frank James turned himself in to the Missouri authorities. He was put on trial in 1883 for the murder of Frank McMillan. The trial was remarkable for two reasons. First, it had to be held in the Gallatin opera house in order to accommodate all the spectators. The people of Clay County, in particular, swarmed into the impromptu courthouse. Second, it suffered from an amazing lack of testimony. Not a single reliable witness could be found for any of the James brothers'

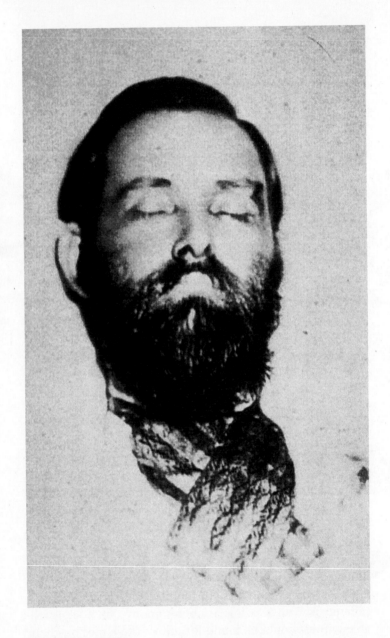

JESSE JAMES IN DEATH

crimes before 1879, and only one witness—Dick Liddil, a band member turned dubious State's evidence—was procured for the crimes after that. Liddil was himself a convict by that time, and his testimony was little use against Frank James, who was acquitted. Later in life, Frank appeared in a Wild West show. He would sit in the shadowy interior of a stagecoach while it was being robbed by actors who shouted out that they were the notorious Frank and Jesse James.

The fates of Jesse's wife, children, mother, step-father and step-siblings are not known. Missouri has produced outstanding individuals in the time since Jesse's death. No one, however, has overtaken the legend of Missouri's most famous son—Jesse James, the family man, the villain—who died, not at the end of a rope or in a federal jail, but within the walls of his own sweet home.

BILLY THE KID

6

Billy the Kid

Billy was gone. Given the heavy, locked doors
of the jail, it appeared at first that he
had simply vanished into thin air.

He died at the age of 21, and legend says he killed as many men as he lived years. Actually, Henry McCarty alias William Bonney alias Billy the Kid probably killed no more than eight people, but the discrepancy points out the single most important thing about him now. Ever since Sheriff Pat Garrett gunned down the youthful outlaw of New Mexico, legend has so intermingled itself with fact that the life of Billy the Kid has become an inseparable mixture of both. Garrett's bullet marked the end of one Billy and the beginning of the next, for since his death, Billy the Kid has surely become the best-loved outlaw of the West.

The origin of the Kid's life is hard to trace. Legend and myth, not to mention sloppy records, cloak the immortal gunslinger. His life probably began in an Irish area of New York City in 1859, when he was born to a Catherine McCarty and christened Henry. He was one of two children, but whether his brother Joe was older or younger than him is not known. One might imagine that a birth record would nail down exactly when and where Billy the Kid entered the world as Henry McCarty; the problem is that more than one Catherine McCarty of Irish descent gave birth around that time to sons whom she named Henry and Joseph. Billy's father has never been certainly identified.

At the end of the Civil War, our Catherine McCarty went to Indianapolis, Indiana, where she met William Antrim, her future husband. Both Antrim and the McCartys moved on to Wichita, Kansas in 1870, where Catherine set up a laundry business while William built a cabin on the edge of town. Not long after that, both the successful business and the cabin were abandoned. The doctor had told Catherine that she had tuberculosis and should move to a warmer, drier clime.

On March 1, 1873, William Antrim and Catherine McCarty got married. The ceremony took place in Santa Fe while they were en route to Silver City. Besides making their love official, the wedding of William and Catherine provided one of the first official and incontrovertible records of Billy the Kid's life. Along with his brother Joe, he was a witness to the ceremony and signed his name—Henry McCarty—in the register handed to him by the Presbyterian minister.

The Antrims (the marriage added yet another knot to Billy's string of names) settled in Silver City in the territory of New Mexico. Silver City was a bustling frontier town. Mining activity had taken off in 1870, and the influx of Anglo-Americans had created a curious feature in the southwestern landscape. On the main street, stately Yankee buildings made of brick reared up out of a ground that had only known Apache wickiups and Mexican adobe huts a few short years before. English-speaking miners, ranchers and cowboys were in the majority, but it was not uncommon for Mexican traders and Native Indians to be seen trudging through the streets. The cultural diversity was a strong influence on young Billy, who developed a good command of Spanish.

William Antrim made his bread and butter by working the mines, and Catherine made space in their cabin for boarders, to bring in extra cash. Billy, for his part, went to school like any other kid. He distinguished himself in singing and dancing, and became an avid reader.

On September 16, 1874, Catherine Antrim succumbed to her disease and died. Her passage out of the world so soon after her marriage changed the course of Billy's life forever. William Antrim was not an insensitive father, but his work did not leave him much time for the children. Billy found a companion in an old drunk named Sombrero Jack. It was Jack that put Billy up to robbing the Chinese laundry; Jack, of course, was nowhere to be found when Billy was caught. The sheriff put the 15-year-old boy in the local jail to teach him a lesson, but when he came to release him, Billy was gone. Given the heavy, locked doors of the jail, it appeared at first that he had simply vanished into thin air.

Billy had just executed the first of the many daring escapes that would make him famous. As soon as he had been left alone, he had crawled into the fireplace and wiggled his way up the chimney. Once free, he lit out for Arizona.

He found work on a ranch for a time, but soon fell in with a bunch of cattle rustlers. As he learned the ropes, he was often caught and often escaped. Once, he threw salt in the eyes of

his guard in order to make a break for it. As the months wore
on, Billy the Kid drifted further and further away from the
straight and narrow, and closer to complete reliance on a fast
horse and a sharp gun. In 1877 at Camp Grant, a fort established to control the Apache Indians, Billy the Kid murdered
his first man.

If the 17-year-old Billy had stuck around after the incident, he
probably would have been acquitted. Francis P. Cahill, the
blacksmith at Camp Grant, had bullied Billy ever since the
latter had come to the Camp. One day Cahill slapped him
once too often, and panicked when he saw Billy go for his
gun. Cahill tackled him, but Billy launched a shot point-blank
into Cahill's belly. The blacksmith died the next day. Instead
of explaining his action, Billy fled back toward the state border. After the murder, he left the name Antrim behind, and
started calling himself William Bonney.

When Billy resurfaced in New Mexico, it was in the company
of the notorious outlaw Jesse Evans. Evans was a hooligan
and a thug, and he is generally credited with cementing the
criminal element in Billy's character. While riding with
Evans, Billy learned to ambush and prey on lone travelers.
He also developed the skill—practiced by the Apache—of
leaning off the side of his horse while it ran at a full gallop.
From this precarious position, he could snatch objects off the
ground or open fire on an unsuspecting target. His relationship to Evans was of mutual benefit: when Evans was jailed
at Lincoln in November 1877 for cattle theft, Billy the Kid
helped break him out.

Evans was a drifter, and he worked at whatever would pay
him. After the jailbreak, he made himself scarce for a while.
Billy remained in Lincoln. Some time in December, he

hired on to the ranch owned by the Englishman John Henry Tunstall.

As far as personalities go, Tunstall was quite the gem. He had a fiery temper and a decent sense of justice. His photograph shows a handsome, intelligent man, whose hair the winds of the frontier sweep back in dashing waves. Born and educated in England, he had come to the Lincoln area in the fall of 1876 to make money ranching. He was only 24 years old when Billy came into his world, but he was already one of the few wealthy people in the area. His ranch lay up against the mountains some 30 miles south of Lincoln, and in addition to the ranch, he owned a store in Lincoln. His chief ambition was to wrest economic control of Lincoln away from a group known as "the House."

The chief figures of the House were Lawrence G. Murphy and Jimmy Dolan. Murphy had a ranch high in the mountain country 20 miles west of Lincoln. He was a ruthless entrepreneur who turned up in New Mexico at the end of the Civil War and began monopolizing the supply of beef to the U.S. Army at Fort Stanton and to the Mescalero Indians. In 1873, the Army got fed up with Murphy's profiteering and gave him the boot. They did not kick him far: he set up shop in Lincoln, and began once more to consolidate his power. Sheriff William Brady of Lincoln virtually became Murphy's henchman. By the time Billy arrived in the area, Murphy felt powerful enough to withdraw into private luxury, and he let his young protégé Jimmy Dolan take over the details of the operation.

Tunstall's allies against the House were Alex McSween and the poorer people of the region who were eager to see a brave young man take on Murphy. McSween was the only lawyer in Lincoln and also operated a store. Tunstall was also

LINCOLN, NEW MEXICO, CA 1886. THE MURPHY-DOLAN STORE IS THE
TWO-STORY STRUCTURE IN THE CENTER.

loosely connected with the great Texas cattle baron, John
Chisum. Chisum had been the first big rancher in New
Mexico and was still considered the king of ranching in the
territory. He had over 100 cowboys in his service, and 80,000
head of cattle. His 150-mile-long ranch lay far to the east of
Lincoln, on the Pecos River. His interest was a long way from
Lincoln, too: when the fighting broke out in 1878, he took no
part in it.

Billy the Kid revered John Tunstall. Legend claims that they became the best of friends after Billy was hired; fact suggests that Tunstall was a busy, important man whom Billy intensely admired. Either way, Tunstall was everything that Billy wanted to be. He was articulate, educated and graceful. Furthermore, he owned his own ranch. Knowingly or not, Tunstall gave direction to Billy's life, and Billy returned the gift with incredible loyalty.

No. 486.

The problems in Lincoln became acute in February 1878. A convoluted legal case involving a life insurance policy brought the conflict to a head, and saw McSween face off against Dolan before Judge Warren Bristol in the courthouse in Mesilla. The upshot was that Sheriff Brady was instructed to impound the property of Alex McSween in the amount of $10,000. Brady executed the command with relish. He moved in on McSween's store with an occupying force and began an inventory. Brady also sent some men off to collect nine of McSween's horses that were then at Tunstall's ranch. When Tunstall heard that a hostile posse had set out for his ranch, he decided to ride for Lincoln, 30 miles to the north, where he would be more secure. Surely the matter could be decided in a civilized fashion? He, Billy and three others drove the nine horses before them.

The posse was a bunch of thugs hired by Dolan to enforce his will. Jesse Evans was among them. So too was a man named Billy Morton. No one, including Tunstall, doubted what the outcome would be if Tunstall went up against Morton and Evans. When the posse got to the ranch and realized that Tunstall had escaped, Morton and Evans recruited a dozen of the fastest men and raced back toward Lincoln.

Meanwhile, in order to keep track of the horses in the rolling landscape, Tunstall and his men were riding at quite a distance from each other. Billy and a man named Middleton were bringing up the rear; they were the first to see Evans's posse crest the ridge behind them. Both sides panicked when the enemy came in sight. A confrontation with his old associate must have sent a cold thrill down Billy's spine. Middleton shot off down the valley to warn Tunstall, while Billy angled up the hillside toward the others, shouting for Middleton to join them as soon as possible. He had hardly reached the others when the hail of bullets hit.

Disadvantaged by the confusion, Billy and the other two men scrambled for the shelter of a few trees and rocks near the top of the hill. By the time they had regrouped, Evans and his band of hungry sharks had swept past them. Ominous shots echoed in the deep recesses of the valley. Billy fretted with anxiety. Outnumbered, they could hardly attack the posse. The most they could hope for was to make a stand and drive off their assailants. More shots were fired. Where was Middleton?

Gradually, the last of the shots echoed away into the gray sky, and there was a faint sound of pounding hoofs. A pall of silence fell upon the land. Suddenly a rider approached. It was Middleton. The flanks of his horse were wet with sweat.

"They've killed Tunstall," he said bluntly.

The murder of John Tunstall sparked the Lincoln County War. The war raged over five months, dove into countless legal entanglements and claimed a number of lives, but in its hottest moment it focused on the figure of a single man and his vow of vengeance. "I'll get some of them before I die," Billy the Kid is reputed to have said, while standing over the body of Tunstall.

And he did. Shortly after the murder, McSween drew up a legal writ to commission a band of his crusaders to hunt down Tunstall's killers. The writ was signed by an old justice of the peace, John B. Wilson. The crusaders called themselves "the Regulators" and adopted vigilante-like tactics, including oaths of allegiance and silence. Billy the Kid was the most ardent of the Regulators. Charley Bowdre, Fred Waite, Doc Scurlock, the Coe brothers, Jim French and John Middleton rode at his side. The band was led by a loyal follower of McSween, Dick Brewer.

When the Regulators caught up to Billy Morton near the Pecos River, an all-out chase ensued. Morton and his companion, Frank Baker, fled as soon as they recognized Brewer, but the Regulators thundered after them with the determination of a locomotive. Round after round of ammunition was discharged as the combatants raced across the plain, but the chase did not end until the horses of the pursued men collapsed in exhaustion. The afternoon sun glinted off the frothy necks of the broken animals. Morton and Baker stumbled into a dip to defend themselves, but surrendered when Dick Brewer gave them a choice. Billy was all for executing them on the spot, but Brewer wanted to deliver them alive to McSween and the machinations of justice.

Captives and captors alike spent the night at John Chisum's ranch. Morton penned a letter to a friend in Virginia, asking him to investigate the matter if Morton mysteriously died before reaching Lincoln.

The letter proved prophetic. On a lonely trail in the Blackwater Ravine, Morton and Baker were shot and killed. Eleven bullets were found in their bodies, one for each of the Regulators. The Regulators claimed that the prisoners had tried to escape.

Sheriff William Brady was the next to fall prey to the Regulators' campaign of revenge. His death shouted out loud and clear that the people had more than a simple vendetta on their hands. Since the impounding of McSween's property had not worked out, Brady now had a warrant for McSween's arrest. Rather than let their leader be held in the enemy's jail, where brutes like Jesse Evans would have their way with him, the Regulators decided to strike first.

On the morning of April 1, 1878, Sheriff Brady was walking up the main street of Lincoln with four of his men, after having taken care of some business at the courthouse. They were just passing the Tunstall store when a party of assassins rose up from behind a low wall with raised rifles. All six Regulators had Brady in their sights when they fired. The bullets knifed through the bright morning air and brutally mowed down the sheriff. His men dove for cover, but one of them was also caught in the murderous stream of lead.

As quickly as it had begun, the firing stopped, and Billy dashed out into the street. Brady was dead, and Billy wanted his rifle. He also had orders to get the arrest warrant that threatened McSween out of the dead man's pocket. Brady's men regrouped and drove the vultures off the carcass: taking a bullet in the thigh, Billy was forced to retreat empty-handed. Later that day, the Regulators slipped out of town unmolested.

Skirmishes occurred through spring and early summer, whenever the sides chanced across each other's path in the sparsely populated county. Dick Brewer was killed in a shoot-out at Blazer's Mills, as was Buckshot Roberts, who had ridden with the posse that killed Tunstall. In late April, Regulators Frank McNab and Ab Saunders were ambushed downstream of Lincoln and killed by a House hitman named Manuel Segovia. On May 15, the Regulators struck back by capturing Segovia; according to his captors, he was killed because he tried to escape. A young man named Tom O'Folliard came to Lincoln looking for work. Billy instantly made a warrior out of him, and Tom became his right-hand man. As the days grew longer, the opponents entrenched themselves deeper and deeper, and prepared for the final showdown.

It came in July.

The Five-Day Battle of Lincoln was precipitated by Alex McSween. After the death of Brady and the unsuccessful attempt to get hold of the warrant for his arrest, McSween had stood trial on old charges involving the life insurance case from February. He had been acquitted by the jury, despite the obvious bias of Judge Bristol against him. Dolan was infuriated by the defeat. He lobbied the territorial governor for a new sheriff, one who would clamp down on the chaos in Lincoln with an iron hand and put a stop to the aggravating Regulators. He got his man in Sheriff George W. Peppin. Peppin had long been loyal to Dolan, and when McSween heard the news, he took to his heels and joined his roaming army in the bush. But McSween overestimated his own love of nature. He was a city slicker through and through. He soon tired of the two things certain in the guerrillas' way of life—dirt and danger—and led his men back to his house in Lincoln, there to force the decisive battle on cleaner terms.

They took up position in McSween's large, adobe house on July 14, 1878. The house stood on the north side of the street. It looked south at some scattered dwellings and the sharply rising hills beyond them. Behind the McSween house was a small yard, beyond which the land sloped gradually down to the river and the trees on its banks. The path through the yard to the river was not a long one—or would not have been a long one, in peacetime.

By afternoon the next day, Sheriff Peppin had found out that McSween and the Regulators were in town. He and his 40 men took up defensive positions around the sprawling, one-story house, and the final battle of the Lincoln County War began.

It began as a stalemate. Each side knew its enemy well, and neither wanted to make a risky move that would foolishly risk lives. The Regulators had had a whole day to fortify the house into a stronghold; followers of the House, by contrast, had the freedom to entrench themselves in regular defenses around their target. Shots were fired and men were killed by the stray bullets, but both forces seemed to be waiting for something more to happen. One day one of the Regulators caught sight of a horseman coming up the road from Fort Stanton. The gunman took aim and fired casually, without much thought of who it could be. The horseman was knocked off his horse, and quickly rode back in the direction he had come.

The thoughtless firing on an unidentified party proved to be a grave mistake.

On the morning of July 19, five days into the siege, Colonel Nathan A.M. Dudley led a dozen cavalrymen and two dozen foot soldiers into Lincoln. They dragged two ominous pieces of heavy machinery behind them. One was a howitzer cannon. The other was a Gatling gun. Dudley proclaimed his position of armed neutrality, explained he had come to protect the women and children of Lincoln from irresponsible warfare, and added that if anyone dared attack the U.S. Army again, the U.S. Army would attack him. Then he trained the Gatling gun on the McSween house and went over to the Wortley Hotel to have lunch.

Peppin's men put their advantage to good use. Covered by the threat of insuperable gunpower, they raided the outermost room of the house—the kitchen—and set it on fire. Much of the house was clay, so the arsonists had some trouble getting a convincing blaze going, but their efforts ultimately rewarded them. By dusk, a voracious inferno was consuming the house, room by room.

McSween was a wreck. He sat in despair, watching his men try to keep the flames from spreading. The smoky darkness corresponded exactly to his mood. His wife had fled. His career was in shambles. He was reduced to relying on a band of gunmen to defend him and his interests. With no thought to the morale of the men under him, he let his head sink to his chest. There he sat in morose despondency until roused by Billy.

"Mr. McSween! Come with me, sir! We're gonna make a break for it."

McSween hardly acknowledged him. His problems were larger than any pistol-twirling kid could solve. The smoke was hissing through the door like steam from a kettle. It swirled above McSween's head.

"Mr. McSween!" Billy's call had more force than before. He kneeled down under the lawyer to catch a look from his sunken face. "Mr. McSween!" Billy reached out to grasp the front of the other man's shirt. Except for the bright red cracks in the doorway off to his right, everything was cloaked in oily, inky blackness. A low, hot sound like the roar of an immense engine engulfed all other noise. Darkness would have fallen across the yard by now too, and the men would be waiting. Waiting for Billy and their leader. Why would the lawyer not rise?

Then Billy understood. No one really believed that a man could escape up a chimney unless he saw it done. He rose and fastened his grasp firmly on McSween's shoulders.

"McSween," he ordered. "Get up."

He did not wait for a response. Holding his breath, he dragged the coughing man out of the room.

The others were waiting in the last room free of flames and smoke. They were peering out into the night. They could not see their enemies, but that was exactly their point of advantage, for neither could their enemies see them. The fire was not yet bright enough to illuminate this last corner of the yard or the path down to the river.

Jim French began the escape. He crept out the door and vanished. Harvey Morris glided out after him, followed by Tom O'Folliard. One by one, the men fled the house like rats from a sinking ship, and swam out into the pitch black night. The Regulators' oath of secrecy had never been as real as in that moment, when they silently slid out the back door of certain death.

Suddenly a patch of roof caved in to the avid fire and a column of flame burst up into the sky. Lurid and diabolic, the tongues of light spat out billows of black and greasy smoke. They lit up the yard: like the treacherous tongue of an informant, the flames fully exposed Billy's men to the sheriff's guns. The final leap for freedom had begun.

With blazing guns, the Regulators dashed for the gate. Peppin's men ran for it too, all the while firing insanely at the ragged, dancing shadows racing beside them. Five men made it out of the yard into the secrecy of the outer darkness. Tom O'Folliard was one. Billy the Kid was another. They careened down to the river, stumbling as they ran, rolling when they fell, and escaped.

Alex McSween did not get to the gate before it was blocked. He scampered back to the burning building when he saw that escape was impossible. A confused call of surrender characterized his last moments. The sheriff's shots delivered a speedy reply. He was struck once, twice, three times, and again and again as he toppled to his doom. The sheriff's posse plugged him with bullets—one for each of the men who had escaped. Punctured with shots, he lay in his yard, looked up at the suffocating smoke, and died.

As Alex McSween's life came crashing to a halt, the curtains were drawn on the terrible Five-Day Battle of Lincoln. Half a dozen men fell victim to its slaughter, the U.S. Army had been provoked into occupying Lincoln, and the mantle of leadership had passed from a wily rebel lawyer to a brazen, unstoppable young man.

Billy the Kid had come of age.

Not all of the Regulators had been in the McSween house, but the band gradually dissolved nonetheless as the year wore on. Charley Bowdre and Doc Scurlock settled in Fort Sumner. Frank Coe and his brother George headed for Colorado. Billy and Tom O'Folliard wandered as far east as Texas and as far north as Las Vegas. They spent some time in Fort Sumner, where Billy got to know a former buffalo hunter named Pat Garrett. Ultimately, Billy could not resist the pull toward Lincoln, which was the area he knew and loved best.

Lincoln knew Billy the Kid, but was split on the question of love. Most of the Hispanic population adored the friendly, nimble dancer who spoke Spanish so fluently. Billy undoubtedly had a number of romantic liaisons during his short adult life. Colonel Dudley, Jimmy Dolan, Jesse Evans and another man of the Dolan faction, Billy Campbell, were not so enthused about the return of Billy the Kid.

Nevertheless, both sides were willing to try peace. The people of Lincoln were tired of violence. On February 18, 1879, the two sides gathered across from each other on Lincoln's main street. Using adobe walls as cover, they kept out of sight at first, but when they were both assured that everyone present desired a truce, they walked out into the street and met face to face. The fugitive Billy the Kid shook hands with the bankrupt Jimmy Dolan, and the two men agreed to get along. No one would attack or testify against his former enemy. After the deal was struck, the two sides went off to drown past hostilities in liquor.

Billy the Kid did not drink, and he saw clearly what happened next.

Sue McSween, the wife of the late Alex, had returned to Lincoln in autumn in the company of a fractious old lawyer named Huston Chapman. All things considered, Chapman was a blustering fool. He took on Sue McSween's case and made her injuries his own. He would have fit right in had he come to Lincoln County a year earlier, but much had happened since the feud had begun, and most people were now willing quietly to accept past wrongs in order to forge future rights. Chapman made no friends by stirring things up again.

Very bad luck put Chapman on the street that night, when a drunken crowd of veterans was lurching from drinking hole to drinking hole. He stumbled into the midst of the warriors. Dolan's man Campbell blocked Chapman's path and poked Chapman's chest with his pistol.

"Dance," he said.

"Am I talking to Mr. Dolan?" Chapman haughtily asked.

"No," came the reply, "but you are talking to a damn good friend of his."

Then, just for fun, Jimmy Dolan drew his pistol, let out a drunken shout and fired at the sky. Campbell jumped at the sound and pulled his trigger. Huston Chapman was blown away, adding yet another name to the list of victims of the Lincoln County War.

When Governor Lew Wallace heard of the murder, he made arrangements finally to visit Lincoln. Wallace is best remembered as the author of the epic *Ben Hur*, but before retreating fully into literary seclusion, he made a weak attempt to end the bloodshed in his territory. In October 1878, Wallace had proclaimed a general amnesty for all the participants of the Lincoln County War in hopes of quelling the conflict, but when the innocent Chapman died in February 1879, he came to Lincoln himself to see Chapman's killers caught, tried and convicted.

Billy seized the opportunity to shore up his security. Apart from rustling the odd horse, he had not caused any trouble in Lincoln since the Five-Day Battle. Furthermore, there were still charges on his head for the murder of William Brady and, mistakenly, the murder of Buckshot Roberts. Billy wanted his slate wiped clean. He wrote to Governor Wallace, offering to testify against Chapman's murderers in exchange for a pardon.

Wallace took the offer seriously. The latest outbreak of violence, however accidental, had sent the citizens of Lincoln scurrying like mice. For fear of reprisal, no one dared stand up in court as a witness, let alone point a convicting finger at Jimmy Dolan.

No one, that is, except Billy the Kid.

On the night of March 17, 1879, Governor Lew Wallace and Justice John Wilson were sitting in Wilson's parlor when a knock came at the door. Wallace bid the visitor enter. In walked Billy. He laid down his guns when he saw that the two old men were alone. After friendly introductions, the negotiations proceeded apace. Wallace asked Billy to surrender and testify in court against the men who murdered Huston Chapman. Billy refused at first, on the grounds that the thugs of the House would break into the jail and kill him for reneging on their deal. His words were recorded in a letter: "I am not afraid to die like a man fighting but I would not like to be killed like a dog unarmed." Wallace explained that the authorities would make a good show of arresting Billy, so that his testimony would appear involuntary. Naturally, he also assured Billy of protection and amnesty. Billy accepted. The young man shook hands with the old man, and a few days later, on March 21, 1879, the successor of Sheriff Peppin, Sheriff Kimball, arrested Billy the Kid at a house in San Patricio, seven miles southeast of Lincoln.

The bargain should have worked, but Judge Warren Bristol and prosecutor William Rynerson smelled a rat. Governor Wallace was called back up to Santa Fe on important business. Before long, Billy realized that the tables had turned. Dolan and his men went free, and Billy was to face charges of murder. Certainly, he was too young to understand the politicking and maneuvering of such a complex court case. When Wallace left him in the lurch, Billy assumed the deal was off. On June 17, 1879, an embittered Billy the Kid busted out of Lincoln and rode for the open plains.

The next year witnessed his transformation into a hardened criminal. He rustled livestock with business-like efficiency from the Staked Plains of Texas to White Oaks, New Mexico. He picked a fight with his former ally, John Chisum. When he came face to face with a bully named Joe Grant in Hargrove's saloon in Fort Sumner, he made short work of his opponent in a shoot-out.

He became a nation-wide celebrity in November 1880.

Billy, Tom O'Folliard and Charley Bowdre had fallen in with men of bad reputations. Dave Rudabaugh, Tom Pickett and Billy Wilson were used to the hard conditions of frontier life, and Rudabaugh in particular was a seasoned badman. Lawmen in Texas and Kansas, as well as New Mexico, had warrants for his arrest. The group of men was not a gang per se—Bowdre even wanted to turn himself in and make a fresh start—but they were willing to work together when it was necessary. In mid-November 1880, they stole some horses from the ranch of Padre Polaco up near Fort Sumner and drove them over to White Oaks for sale. On their

way back from White Oaks, they spent the night at the shared ranch of "Whiskey Jim" Greathouse and Fred Kuch.

Billy the Kid and Tom O'Folliard must have had a sense of déjà vu when they woke up on the morning of November 27, 1880 to find the house surrounded by a posse.

Deputy Sheriff William H. Hudgeons was at its fore. He sent in a note demanding that the horse rustlers give themselves up. The outlaws laughed, but sent back a note saying that they would discuss the terms of surrender if the lawmen would send in an unarmed negotiator. Whiskey Jim Greathouse was sent out in exchange. As soon as the negotiator, Jimmy Carlyle, entered the house, the rustlers grabbed him and told him that he was their prisoner. They poured him some alcohol and told him to get comfortable.

As the hours wore on, Sheriff Hudgeons began to get nervous. What if the outlaws had simply killed Carlyle? At 2:00 PM, he announced an ultimatum. If Carlyle were not sent out immediately, Greathouse would be killed. It may be that, as in the murder of Huston Chapman, a stray or accidental shot prompted the violence. One of the posse's rifles was discharged. Within moments, Carlyle came crashing out of the window, followed by three speedy bullets. He was dead before he hit the ground.

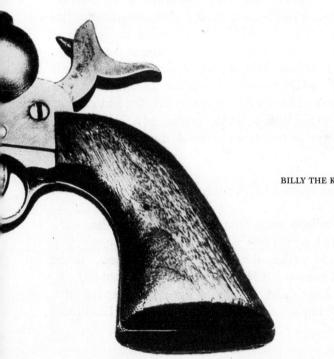

BILLY THE KID'S COLT .44

The killing demoralized the posse utterly. Instead of laying siege to the house with renewed vigor, they backed away from the fight. Probably they were hungry and cold after the long wait. Whatever the reason, they let Billy the Kid and the other outlaws escape.

The killing of the well-liked Carlyle touched off indignation among the residents of White Oaks. Unlike other moments of indignation, this one coincided with an event in the press. Prompted by powerful cattle owners, the *Las Vegas Gazette* had been preparing a detailed report of criminal act-ivity in New Mexico and was on the verge of publishing it when the news came in from White Oaks. The editor at the Gazette took the names of the rustlers and pasted them into his article: one "Billy the Kid" was identified as being the ringleader of the felons who were hindering the economic development of New Mexico. Billy's name spread through the press like wildfire, and on December 27, 1880, the *New York Sun* carried a full-length feature on Billy the Kid, chief of the outlaws of the Wild West. In the space of a single month, Billy shot from obscurity to national, if not international, fame.

He had seven months left to enjoy it.

Governor Wallace reacted to the killing in White Oaks with decision. He told the newly elected sheriff of Lincoln, Pat Garrett, to get the Kid at whatever cost. Governor Wallace also put out a reward of $500 for anyone who could bring in Billy the Kid, dead or alive. Garrett accepted the assignment. He knew Billy from Fort Sumner. The chase was on.

Garrett went after the Kid relentlessly. With the help of the Azariah Wild, a special operative of the U.S. Secret Service, Garrett tracked the Kid like a bloodhound.

On December 19, 1880, Garrett and his men lured Billy and his men into Fort Sumner. The ambush was sprung a little too soon, and most of the men got away. Tom O'Folliard was not one of the lucky ones. He was shot in the chest. Garrett's men brought him inside and laid him on a bed. Garrett stood by his side as he died.

Garrett and his men were on to Billy. On December 23, 1880, they saddled up and rode out into the pristine, moonlit night. A crisp snow covered the ground and clearly showed the tracks of some horsemen leading east. Garrett and his posse followed the trail to an abandoned farmhouse at a place called Stinking Springs. The outlaws could be heard snoring. After a brief argument over the best course of action to follow, the lawmen surrounded the house and waited for daylight.

When dawn came, a man in a sombrero came out of the house. The posse took aim with their rifles, and fired. Charley Bowdre was hit by half a dozen bullets at once. Mortally wounded, he fell back into the house. The lawmen were close enough to hear what next was said among the outlaws. Billy told Bowdre that the wounds were bad, very bad, but urged him to make a show of surrendering and pick off some of the lawmen before he died. Charley Bowdre was then unceremoniously dumped out the front door. He staggered toward Garrett, but died before he could effect any damage.

Pat Garrett was a patient man. Rather than storm the house and risk the lives of his men, he merely waited until the outlaws realized that they were hopelessly trapped. At 4:00 PM, his patience was rewarded. Billy the Kid, Dave Rudabaugh, Tom Pickett and Billy Wilson limped out of the house with their hands up. They were thirsty and weak with hunger. Garrett arrested them all immediately and brought them back to Santa Fe.

Billy was transferred to Mesilla to stand trial for the murder of Sheriff Brady. The presiding judge was none other than his old foe, Warren Bristol. Influenced by a long speech by the judge, the jury quickly returned a guilty verdict. On April 13, 1881, Billy the Kid was sentenced to death.

After the courtroom had quieted down and the prisoner was led away, a reporter from the *Mesilla News* got a brief interview with the infamous outlaw. "I think it hard I should be the only one to suffer the extreme penalty of the law," Billy said, referring to the Lincoln County War.

A company of guards, including William Mathews, John Kinney and Bob Olinger, escorted the Kid back to Lincoln. Billy's hands and feet were manacled before he was locked in a room in the old Murphy-Dolan store on the west edge of town. On April 28, 1881, the day on which Garrett left town to finalize the details of the execution, Billy surprised his enemies yet again, and broke out of prison.

James W. Bell was on guard on the evening when the Kid made his break. He and Bell were just returning from the outhouse, when Billy, despite his shackles and handcuffs, scampered up the stairs. Panting, Bell lumbered after him, but at the top of the stairs he was dealt a stunning blow across the face. Billy, whose hands were slimmer than his wrists, had slipped out of the cuffs and used them as a cruel whip. Prisoner and guard struggled until at last Billy got hold of Bell's pistol, and shot him.

Billy's hands were free. He was armed. He dragged himself across the floor to the window where he saw Olinger running toward the store. He called out to him from above. The surprised Olinger stopped, looked up and was sent hurtling into eternity by Billy's bullet. Billy the Kid had just killed his last man.

Out of fear, an old acquaintance helped Billy smash the irons from his legs and gave him a horse. The citizens of Lincoln watched him go. Most still knew and liked him.

Billy galloped out of Lincoln two weeks before his date with the hangman. His escape was trumpeted in the press. Panicking, many newspapermen opined that Billy the Kid could not be brought down by the forces of justice, that he was a superhuman force too big to be stopped.

When Sheriff Garrett heard the news, he is reputed to have said, "Now I have to capture him all over again." Despite his repeated warnings to Bell and Olinger, the Kid had slipped through their fingers. Garrett prided himself on his belief in the fairness and impartiality of justice, and felt it his duty to uphold the laws of New Mexico at whatever cost. He began tracking the Kid again.

For three months he rode the ranges of New Mexico; for three months, Billy eluded him. Finally, on the moonlit night of July 14, 1881, Garrett rode into Fort Sumner. After a fruitless search, he and his men reined up before the house of Pete Maxwell. Fort Sumner had been plunged into a particularly dark night. Only a sliver of moonlight cast its pale glow on the hot town. Leaving his men Poe and McKinney outside, Garrett slipped into the house to ask Maxwell if he knew where Billy was.

Maxwell was asleep. The lights were out.

Maxwell, when woken and asked, said that he had not seen Billy.

Meanwhile, outside, a figure walked toward Poe and McKinney. The men watched him approach. The figure was wearing neither shoes nor a hat, and only realized that he was being watched at the last moment.

He sprang back from the lawmen and hissed, "Quien es?"

Poe and McKinney did not identify themselves. The figure repeated his demand as he backed into Maxwell's house.

Garrett was sitting in the darkness at the head of Maxwell's bed, wondering what to do next, when a dark shape entered the room and asked, "Maxwell, who are those men outside?"

Maxwell gulped. "That's him!" he sputtered.

Garrett was caught by complete surprise. He fumbled for his gun. The newcomer became aware of the dark shape at Maxwell's side only then. "Quien es?" he asked again, stepping backward, drawing his weapon.

A brilliant white blast exploded in the darkness, blinding all three men.

The heavy darkness was thrown aside only for a moment. Immediately it clamped down on the room again.

Garrett cocked his pistol and fired again. He heard a groan, but had lost all sight of his target. Following a terrified Maxwell, he stumbled outside, shouting at his men not to shoot.

"I think I got him," he said. "I think I've killed Billy the Kid."

"Are you sure?" McKinney asked dubiously.

Garrett did not answer. Maxwell ran next door to get a candle, and quickly returned. Cautiously he stepped up to the window and looked inside.

The flickering circle of light showed the body of a young man lying on the floor. In his right hand was a pistol. In his left was a knife. He was dead.

It was indeed Billy the Kid.

Sheriff Garrett was baffled. The outcome seemed somehow impossible. He and his men kept quiet that night. A strange fear flowed darkly through the town. None of the men slept. Strange faces bobbed past the Maxwell house, and Garrett and his men were forced to keep up a constant guard, for fear of reprisal.

The next morning, daylight put their fears to rest. The body was identified. Indeed, the youthful body of Billy the Kid was dead, but the reputation had already climbed into immortality. Garrett's bullet marked the birth of a huge legend. Billy was buried beside two of his gang, Tom O'Folliard and Charley Bowdre. An unostentatious tombstone bore the single word, "Pals."

Within six weeks of his death on July 14, a book called *The True Life of Billy the Kid* was being sold on the streets of New York City. Billy the Kid had finally shaken off the bonds of one life, and escaped into another.

BLACK BART

7

Black Bart

He was meticulous, organized and efficient.
He eluded capture masterfully.
Most notably of all, he possessed a sense of humor.

harles Bolton was a gentleman. He took to robbery late in life, apparently coming to believe that he could make more money as a highwayman than from honest living. Operating in California between 1875 and 1883, the solo bandit robbed over two dozen stagecoaches without firing a single shot in anger or defense. On a couple of occasions he left doggerel pieces of verse signed "Black Bart, the PO-8," and thereby endeared himself to the newspapermen of California. He was the master of the lone stagecoach holdup, and truly a man of style.

His real name was probably Charles E. Boles, but he went by the name of Bolton. He was an Easterner, born and raised in upper New York State. When the Civil War broke out, he left a wife and three children and moved to Illinois, where he served on the Union side as a sergeant in the 116th Illinois

Volunteer Infantry. After the war, heartsick and disillusioned by the squalor and misery of the conflict, Bolton may have reunited with his wife and children briefly, but he did not stay with them long. He drifted west to California, where the tantalizing promise of untold riches made many a heart beat faster. But, as many before him had learned, the lure of gold turned out to be false.

Bolton moved from job to job, working in mining before choosing the free life of a general roustabout. Money was always a problem. What was a gentleman to do when times got hard?

The State of California, and particularly the Wells Fargo Stagecoach Company, would soon find out.

The day of July 26, 1875 was overcast and muggy. The Wells Fargo stagecoach moved slowly along the mountain road that wound its way up Funk Hill. Streaks of dust stuck to the sides of the coach. The driver jounced and jostled as the team of horses strained forward through the close heat. The rocks dislodged by their hooves clattered and trickled down the steep embankment like a presentiment of rain. The road twisted intricately, and driver John Shines, who would later serve as both a U.S. marshal and a State senator, tugged hard on the reins to steer the horses cautiously at a crawling pace into each bend.

A couple of seconds later the coach stopped completely. Shines stared at a tall individual in a long dun-colored duster standing in the middle of the road. A white flour sack with eyeholes cut out covered his head and face. Most importantly, the figure wielded a shotgun menacingly.

"Throw down your box!" The bandit's voice was deep and resonant. The muggy stillness was disturbed only by the skittish horses champing at their bits as dust billowed from under their hooves. Driver Shines stared hard at the hooded robber, who, cradling his shotgun, had fallen silent after barking his single command. Without a word, Shines reached under his seat and threw the strongbox onto the road in front of the stagecoach. It contained over $2000. Dust shot from under the padlocked wooden box when it landed hard at the feet of the bandit. He waited for the dust to settle and motioned with his shotgun for the stage to proceed.

After the stagecoach vanished around a bend, the masked man bent and dragged the strongbox away.

Shines stopped the stage a little way down the road. He was about four miles outside of Copperopolis. Instead of going on to town directly, Shines wanted to make sure that he wasn't succumbing to heat stroke or hallucinations. The ghostly figure, though menacing, had been puzzling, even surreal. The robbery had taken place so quickly that Shines needed to reassure himself that it had actually happened. He walked back to where the road began to curve, scanning the woods and rocky outcrops. Suddenly he stopped stock-still, seeing six rifles trained on him by bandits hiding behind boulders. Shines raised his hands. Pinned by fear, he awaited their will. Then he looked harder and lowered his hands. The bandits did not move. He walked to the side of the road and gasped. The rifles were sticks propped on dummies. Relieved, he knocked the hat off of one dummy. He trudged back to the stagecoach, pondering the unusual robbery, and then climbed up and continued apace to report the holdup.

So began the criminal career of the man who would become known as Black Bart or "The Gentleman Robber." His method of operating would vary little over the next few years. Black Bart always robbed stagecoaches. He always picked treacherous roads that were high in the mountains, little traveled, narrow, full of curves and twists and bends, and desolate. His costume remained the same: he always wore a long duster, which reached below his knees and had once been white but was now stained to a mottled beige, and a white sack with eyeholes. He always carried a shotgun. He said little besides commanding stagecoach drivers to toss down their strongboxes. His voice was deep, hollow-sounding and resonant, according to passengers and drivers. He used the ruse of having a few stuffed dummies cover him from the sides of the road, and he sometimes told his inanimate confederates, "If he dares to shoot, give him a solid volley, boys." Each time, after the shadowy bandit had disappeared with the loot, the driver and passengers found that they had been intimidated by a bunch of sacks stuffed with cotton and tied with rope. The one decidedly live figure, however, always seemed to disappear without a trace. Pursuing posses found nothing in the way of clues or leads.

During this time robbers and brigands galore roamed the hills and valleys of California, such that even the solitary nature of this man, his distinctive attire and his novel "gang" might not have marked him for special attention. He might have been just one of many outlaws being pursued by posses and lawmen. But Bolton had style. He was meticulous, organized and efficient. He eluded capture masterfully. Most notably of all, he possessed a sense of humor and a desire to add to his enigmatic persona.

Stagecoach drivers noticed that the lone bandit wore large socks over his boots so as to leave no distinctive heel marks as he made off with the contents of the strongboxes. He also never rode a horse, choosing instead to make his way through the mountainous terrain on foot. He stuffed his coat with whatever the strongbox contained. He later revealed that planning a heist involved walking out to a desolate location, camping overnight in the woods without a fire, caching food, planning the most advantageous place to be positioned, preparing a carefully thought-out escape route for himself and always setting up his decoys with artistry and finesse in advance.

Aside from careful planning and well-honed survival skills, Bolton thwarted capture because his holdups were so sporadic. Although the manner in which they happened seldom varied, they seemed to be committed only when Black Bart needed cash. Sometimes, months elapsed between holdups. In these times, pursuit slackened, then dissolved. Then the strangely dressed but somehow dignified robber would suddenly appear again, standing in the middle of a lonely stretch of mountain road. He would cradle a shotgun, speak brusquely through his disguise and then disappear, as if into thin air.

Following a number of holdups by Bolton in 1875 and 1876, there was a long lull in his activities. Spring and summer passed. The masked robber was absent from the backroads of California. Stagecoach drivers and passengers relaxed. The mysterious outlaw had perhaps moved to a different part of the country? Maybe he had even given up the game of robbery for good.

Then one fine morning in August 1877, the Arena stagecoach set out for Duncan's Mill on the Russian River, north of Santa Rosa. The depot clerk had called out to the driver, "All quiet on the run so far?" and the latter had nodded. "Yeah, it's been real peaceful. Not expecting anything on a day like today." Then the stagecoach had circled, filling the yard with dust.

It wound its way through the sage- and scrub-covered hills. Besides the stagecoach wending its way through the mountains, there was little else in the way of movement. As the driver eased the coach through two enormous boulders, Black Bart stepped onto the road and leveled a shotgun at the driver. The driver started and yanked on the reins, and the horses whinnied and reared. The hooded bandit gave the now familiar command in a polite, but firm, bass: "Throw down your Wells Fargo box, sir!" The driver hoisted the box and threw it to the ground, and alerted the passengers to the situation. They peered out cautiously and were taken aback to see the garish figure. A wave of the shotgun induced them to jerk their heads back into the coach.

"I don't want your money," boomed the masked gunman. "I only want *that.*" He gestured with the barrel of his shotgun to the strongbox on the ground. He motioned the driver on his way, bowed slightly to the female passengers as the stage passed and watched it as it moved off down the road. When the coast was clear, he lugged the strongbox away from the road and escaped.

The take from the robbery was $600. A posse scouring the road and surrounding hills found the Wells Fargo box the next day, not too far from the scene of the crime. It had been emptied of its contents, but contained a scrawled note. It read:

> *I've labored long and hard for bread,*
> *For honor and for riches.*
> *But on my corns too long you've tred,*
> *You fine-haired sons of bitches.*

It was signed "Black Bart, PO-8."

The newspapers eulogized the successful bandit as a gentleman robber who also possessed a sense of humor. The verse did not provide much help to lawmen who were seriously tracking the elusive outlaw, but it did entertain anyone else who came across it, for its mocking lilt made fun of the Wells Fargo Stagecoach Company. The company and lawmen were not amused, especially since they were so powerless to bring the thief to justice. Even less droll were the rumors that said that the stage had been robbed by a ghost. Black Bart's mysterious appearances and disappearances remained unexplained.

Another year passed before Black Bart struck again. This time he robbed the stage traveling between Oroville and Quincy on July 26, 1878. As in all previous holdups, he simply appeared from behind some boulders on the side of the road. He ordered that the strongbox with a little less than $400 in it be handed over, and this time he relieved a passenger of a diamond ring and a watch. He told the driver that his gang would open fire at the first sign of movement, and then vanished behind the boulders.

Lawmen again found the strongbox; it was empty, save for another verse:

> Here I lay me down to sleep
> To wait the coming morrow,
> Perhaps success, perhaps defeat
> And everlasting sorrow.
> Yet come what will, I'll try it once
> My conditions can't be worse,
> And if there's money in that box,
> 'Tis money in my purse.

The penny newspapers in the cities had a field day. The newspapermen reveled in the mysterious ways of the robber, opining that the man was an apparition that materialized and then vanished. Drivers and passengers attested to the courteous manner of the outlaw, his desire to rob Wells Fargo almost exclusively, and his seeming reluctance to use the shotgun he toted. Indeed, in the course of his 29 holdups, Black Bart never fired his weapon. Usually, there was no opposition from the stagecoach drivers or passengers. Most were content to watch as the strangely dressed robber dragged the strongboxes off into the bush.

Not all drivers were of like minds, though, and armed resistance was to be Black Bart's undoing. He continued to rob stagecoaches sporadically, without much variation. On July 13, 1882, George Hackett was driving the Wells Fargo stagecoach outside of the small town of Strawberry. Black Bart jumped out from behind a boulder and stood in front of the stagecoach as it rolled to a stop. Very politely, the bandit said, "Please throw down your strongbox." Instead of complying as all other drivers had in the past, Hackett reached for the rifle strapped beside him, raised it to his waist and casually fired at the masked man before him. The startled bandit bolted for the sanctuary of the woods empty-handed.

Black Bart probably recognized his robbing days were near an end; he certainly did not want to be seriously wounded or killed. The gunfire from the coach driver had unnerved him. He considered himself a gentleman, above the common ruffians. He was not someone who needed to use the weapon he carried.

The lone robber carried off at least one or two more successful robberies of Wells Fargo stagecoaches, but his unwillingness to fire his weapon cost him his career. On

November 3, 1883, he was back on Funk Hill, at almost exactly the spot where his first robbery had occurred over eight years before. As the stagecoach labored around a hairpin turn in the road, Black Bart stepped out and issued his usual order to throw down the strongbox.

The driver ducked out of sight and ran off.

Perplexed by the move, Black Bart climbed up to the driver's seat to look for the Wells Fargo box. It was not there, but he soon found it tightly fastened to the inside of the stagecoach. He began trying to work it loose, but it resisted his efforts. Where had the driver run off to? Grabbing an ax, Black Bart began hacking at the stubborn strongbox.

Just as he was finally getting the strongbox open, a shot ripped into the stagecoach. The driver, whose name was Reason McConnell, had returned with Jimmy Rolleri, a young hunter who had leapt off the stage a short way back to flush out some game with his rifle while the stage labored up the twisting road. Another blast rocked the vehicle. Cursing, Black Bart stuffed what he could of the loot into his pockets, and then rushed outside toward the cover of the rocks. A bullet grazed his knuckle, and he dropped a little bundle—including a handsome handkerchief. He managed to escape into the woods, but for the first time, Black Bart had left a clue.

The two principal lawmen who had been assigned to put an end to the string of robberies were on the scene shortly afterwards. James Hume and Harry Morse soon realized that this was their first tangible lead on Black Bart's identity. The handkerchief bore a San Francisco laundry mark. Morse, determined to find and capture the hooded robber of so many stagecoaches, scoured the San Francisco business directory and counted up 91 laundry facilities. He set out with Hume to visit each and every one.

The painstaking detective work did what armed and mounted posses had not been able to do, and their perseverance was soon rewarded. "Oh yes!" exclaimed the proprietor of one particular laundry shop when Morse visited with the tell-tale handkerchief. "Mr. Bolton has done business with us for a few years now. He's the very essence of a gentleman, tall and courtly." His patter petered out under the steely gaze of the lawman. "I will need the address of his residence," Morse said curtly, leaning over the counter.

Gathering the local constabulary, the two detectives went to Bolton's hotel and placed him under arrest for being Black Bart, the robber of 29 stagecoaches. The outlaw protested his innocence and insisted that he was a gainfully employed mining man named Charles Bolton.

The detectives hauled Black Bart down to the San Francisco county jail. He languished there for a few days before confessing. Hume only got him to confess to the last of his 29 stagecoach robberies.

The infamous hooded bandit was quickly arraigned on charges of highway robbery and placed before a judge in November 1883. He was convicted. In deference to his age, perhaps, and because he had never once resorted to violence in the course of his crimes, the presiding judge sentenced Black Bart to seven years in the San Quentin prison. He arrived at the gates of the imposing structure on November 21, 1883 to begin his sentence.

Bolton had cooperated with Hume and was a model prisoner, so he served only four and a half years of his sentence before being released. But the years in prison took their toll on him. He walked out, blinking in the bright winter sunlight, on January 21, 1888. The tall and proud highwayman was now stooped. He was deaf in one ear, and his vision was failing. His white hair was more a testament to a broken spirit than wisdom. A gaggle of newspaper reporters waited eagerly as he was ushered to the gates. "Have you renounced your criminal ways?" shouted one reporter as the throng surged around him.

"Will you ever rob again?" pressed another.

The broken bandit insisted he was done with holding up stagecoaches and only wanted to live a peaceful life away from all the commotion. He walked, frail and stooped, to a waiting cab, with a particularly persistent cub reporter dogging his footsteps.

"Does this mean you won't be writing any more poems?" he persisted. Black Bart drew himself up to the best of his ability, showing a flash of his former self. A proud and solitary bandit glowered down at the newspaperman. Emphatically, with the booming voice that had commanded many a driver to throw down his strongbox, he retorted acidly, "I told you I have given up crime!" Turning on his heel, he ducked into the cab and retired to his hotel.

The newspapers reveled in the release of Black Bart. Rumors abounded that Wells Fargo had quietly provided the bandit with a pension for life, a sort of independent income, if you please, on the condition that the Gentleman Robber would never prey on their stagecoaches again.

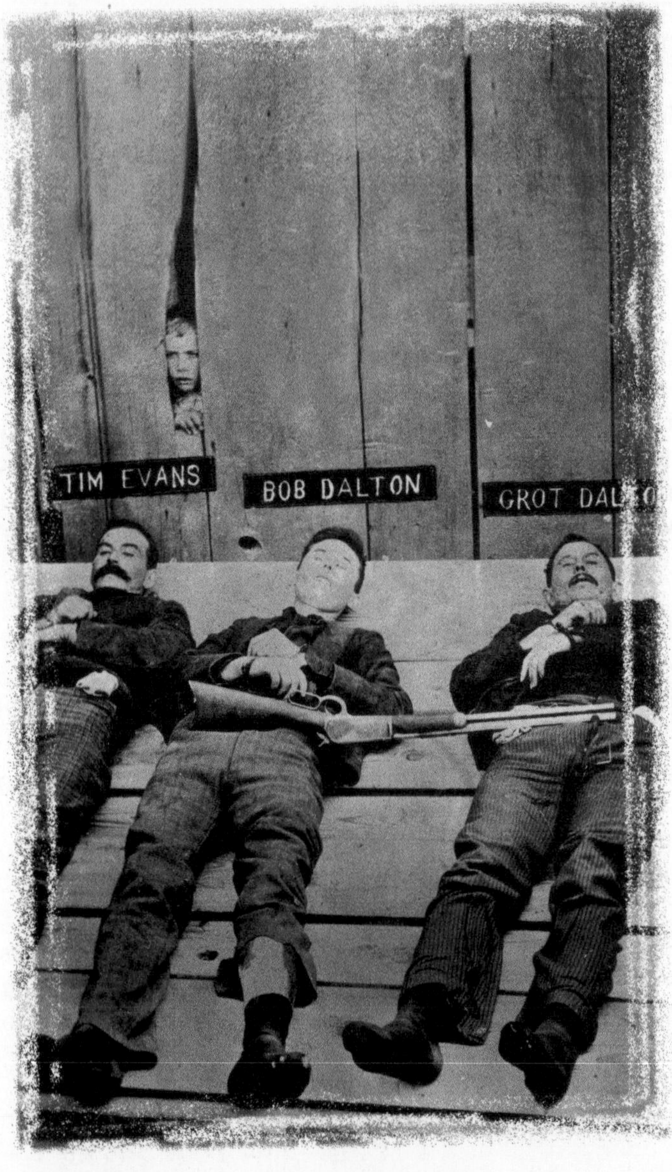

AFTER THE SHOOT-OUT: BILL POWERS, BOB DALTON AND GRAT DALTON.

8

The Dalton Gang

Wealth and fame beckoned. Here was a chance to do something no one else had done. "Our names will go down in history," Bob said as he explained his plan for hitting both banks simultaneously.

Rise and shine, gentlemen," Frank Dalton called out into the gray morning of November 7, 1887. His stentorian voice of authority was swallowed up in the stillness of the little clearing. The fugitives' camp was in disarray, but it was utterly still. "Lee Dixon. Baldy Smith. Get up!" Frank dismounted; as he walked toward the remains of the previous night's campfire, Dixon and Smith began to wake from their stupor—the ground was littered with evidence of wild carousing. Frank towered over the groggy, still prostrate men. He pulled a document from his breast pocket. "Baldy Smith and Lee Dixon, you are charged with illegally trafficking in alcohol." Softening his voice, he added, "Whiskey runnin' ain't never done anyone no good, boys. You ought to know that." He prodded Smith with his boot. "Git up. You're arrested."

By this time, Smith was wide awake. "Who the hell are you?" he croaked, propping himself up on his elbows. The blankets in his makeshift nest were beaded with dew, and his toes were ice cold.

Frank answered, "My name is Frank Dalton. I am a deputy U.S. marshal, an officer of law enforcement." There was a pause as Dixon finally managed to sit up as well. The two men seemed to consider the marshal's declaration for a moment.

Then Dixon responded. His hair was unkempt, and his face unwashed. But his blue eyes were crystal clear. "Why?"

In the corner of his eye, Frank caught sight of a sudden movement in the mist. He looked more carefully into the surrounding trees. Just as he realized how exposed he was—the only standing target in the marshy clearing!—gunfire pierced the morning stillness. A bullet ripped into Frank's stomach. Doubled over in agony, the marshal fumbled with the holster of his six-shooter. He drew the gun and pressed it against his thigh to cock the hammer. His other hand clutched at his bloody belly. He somehow managed to squeeze off a few random shots before slumping to the ground, where he writhed in excruciating pain for a moment.

And then Frank Dalton was dead.

If their older brother Frank had not been murdered, the Dalton family history might have told quite a different story. Bob, Gratton and Emmett—these are the Dalton brothers who achieved infamy and became legends of the Wild West. Their outlaw gang operated in the wilds of present-day Oklahoma and Kansas. Their notoriety rests on their final, audacious plan to rob both of the banks in their hometown of Coffeyville, Kansas in October, 1892; but they were not born outlaws.

The Daltons were the product of an uncertain age, and they grew up in a volatile, poorly defined area. The state where

Emmett Dalton spent most of his life changed its name three times.

The Dalton brothers were born in Missouri. In 1882 the impoverished clan—15 children were born in all—moved to Coffeyville, Kansas, and thereafter to the nearby town of Vinita. The family patriarch, Lewis Dalton, was a shell-shocked veteran of the Mexican War who was given to drinking and gambling with his meager pension. He was exceptionally lazy and did little to support his wife, Adeline, and the ever-increasing brood of children they raised on the hardscrabble, dirt-poor farms to which they moved in spirit-crushing succession.

Vinita is now a town in eastern Oklahoma; at that time, it was still part of Indian Territory, which the government had formed in 1834 as a forced destination point for the Cherokee, Creek, Seminole, Choctaw and Chickasaw Natives who had been displaced by white settlers. The land assigned to them lay west of the Missouri River and north of the Red River, comprising what is now Kansas, Nebraska and Oklahoma. Lofty intentions for the future of the Native Americans had caused the creation of the Territory, but as the 19th century progressed, even these lands began to be settled and used by the whites. In 1854, Kansas and Nebraska were made separate territories; they would soon become states. Oklahoma would not enter the Union until 1907, but the dissolution of the purely "Indian" territory was well underway long before then.

The Daltons came of age during this unstable transformation of Indian Territory. They responded to the rampant lawlessness of the time—first by fighting it, then by embracing it. Frank and Gratton both became deputy U.S. marshals, but on that November day in 1887, Frank was gunned down by the Smith-Dixon Gang. Bob Dalton was 17 when his brother was killed; Emmett was only 15. A year later, Bob leveled a suspected horse thief with a bullet of his own. The murder did not hinder his career. Two years after the death of Frank, Bob also became a deputy marshal. He worked in the Osage Nation, tracking cattle thieves, killers, rustlers and other outlaws.

Frank's death cast a long shadow over his younger brother Bob. Like many desperadoes who start out with good intentions, Bob soon realized that the rewards of enforcing the law paled in comparison to those that could be gained by breaking it. His meager pay, when it was received at all, was hardly the thanks he felt he deserved for exhausting days spent riding in dogged pursuit of criminals. Easier money was surely to be had rustling horses. Bob Dalton quickly convinced his youngest brother, Emmett, to forsake his own tedious job for a more lucrative enterprise. Besides, Bob figured that the work they had put in protecting ranchers and farmers justified the occasional theft of livestock.

In light of Frank Dalton's murder at the hands of bootleggers, the first charge brought against brothers Bob and Emmett was ironic—they were alleged to have sold whiskey to Indians. Emmett was cleared of the charges, but Bob was expected to stand trial. Because the courts were clogged with many more pressing cases, Bob's day in court never arrived and the charges eventually expired.

Bob soon discovered that his older brother Grat was also dissatisfied with his lot in life. Grat was fearless and seemingly impervious to pain, but he was also dull-witted and insensitive. He had nothing against turning to a more profitable profession, whether it was legal or not. Grat had been Bob's superior in the posse that tracked the horse thief whom Bob had shot, but he quickly decided that his younger brother's judgment was to be trusted in most cases. Bob, who already saw himself as responsible for Emmett, now took charge of the burly Grat and emerged as a natural leader. Under Bob's guidance, the three Dalton brothers began a new career as nighttime marauders.

At first, the illicit operation worked well. The Daltons struck shrewdly, stealing good horses as opportunity afforded until they had assembled a valuable herd. They would make regular trips across the border to sell their plundered goods.

In 1890, what remained of Indian Territory was renamed Oklahoma Territory. With the name change, the luck of the horse rustlers took a turn for the worse. A posse surprised the Daltons as they were attempting to sell stolen horses in Kansas and a gunfight ensued. Bob and Emmett escaped unscathed; Grat also avoided injury, but lost his brothers during their frantic escape. The hoofprints of his horse were easily tracked in the soft riverbank mud through which he fled. The posse caught up with him as he was trying to ford the stream. Given the vulnerability of his position, he had no choice but to surrender.

Grat was held in the local jail to await trial, but justice was once again bungled before a Dalton could be brought before a jury. Lack of evidence proving Grat's role in the horse rustling won him his freedom, and he sauntered away from the jail with his hands in his pockets. As soon as he hooked up with Bob and Emmett, they set out for California together. There was no lack of evidence against Bob and Emmett; a flood of wanted posters washed across the Territory as the outlaws sped west. Their plan was to find their brother Bill, who was Bob's senior by seven years and Grat's junior by two. Their journey took them across the Rio Grande and into Silver City, where they sojourned for the summer. They continued west through Arizona territory. The lure of the brothels and saloons along the way frequently hampered their progress, but Bob, Emmett and Grat finally arrived at Bill's home—near Visalia, California—in late 1890.

Bill Dalton was a relatively prosperous farmer and a local politician. Bill's relatives did not receive a very warm welcome from his wife, but the outlaws were heartily greeted by their brother. Bill was well established in Californian society and did not want to join the wandering gang. But he did provide information, legal advice and a place of refuge for his siblings—all the while maintaining an outward show of respectability for the sake of the Dalton name.

In February 1891, Bill's good reputation was stripped away. History has still not decided whether the Daltons were responsible for holding up the Southern Pacific Railroad at Alila, California, on February 6, but observers at the time did not hesitate to pin the crime on Bill Dalton and his suspicious bunch of relatives. Grat was said to be an exact match for the description on the wanted poster, so Detective William Smith arrested Bill and Grat. The latter was convicted of the offense and jailed; Bill was acquitted, but his social standing and family name had been forever tarnished. Once again, Bob and Emmett got away.

They returned to the land they knew best. No one knows exactly how or why good men turn bad, but the transformation of these two was now complete. By the time Bob and Emmett resurfaced in Oklahoma Territory, all vestiges of their law-abiding (much less law-enforcing) past were gone from their characters and unrepentant villainy had taken root. As Bob and Emmett perfected their thieving techniques, they attracted other men of dubious morality. The resulting affiliation of crooks and thieves soon earned unparalleled notoriety among the people of Oklahoma Territory.

The core of the Dalton Gang was made up of the brothers, but it also drew a number of satellite criminals who drifted in and out as necessity dictated; it was an ever-changing conglomeration of thieves and layabouts. They took up residence in a fortified, well-provisioned bunker-like camp on the farm of a fat, balding man known as "Ol' Yountis."

Bill Powers was one of the relatively constant members. He was a tall, engaging Texan who went by half a dozen aliases. He had a certain calm about him and never let himself feel hurried during a robbery. Another steady member of the Dalton Gang was Dick Broadwell, a cowboy who had decided that the life of an outlaw suited him more. He wore a bandanna and played the guitar, but was most remarkable for his soft streak. Whether riding horseback or tending camp, Broadwell always cradled a kitten in his arms.

Other core gang members included George "Bitter Creek" Newcomb, who had drifted into a life of crime after working as a cowboy for various ranchers; Charlie Pierce, who had fled to the Indian Territory from Missouri a few steps ahead of the law; and Bill Doolin, who, after the Coffeyville raid, would team up with a vengeful Bill Dalton to lead the rejuvenated gang on still more robberies. There was also "Blackface" Charley Bryant, who got his nickname from an ugly powder burn on his face. Bryant was extremely self-conscious, and no stranger lived long if he cracked jokes about how the burn marred the outlaw's visage.

Despite the gang's formidable roster, the acknowledged leader remained Bob Dalton. He was a crack marksman and a highly charismatic personality—the latter trait serving him well both as a commander of desperadoes and as a successful ladies' man. Bob knew that there was no going back to former ways, but horse rustling increasingly had its difficulties—not the least of which was finding a place big enough to store the four-legged loot. Angry ranchers kept a sharp lookout for their stolen animals, and the business of eluding the furious posses that strung out through the countryside in pursuit of thieves became more and more difficult. The risk of capture had increased astronomically since the wanted posters had flooded the territory, and the monetary returns from rustling weren't able to satisfy his needs any longer anyway. Bob began to look around for better uses of his time. He would prefer something that didn't involve having to hide out for so long before cashing in the stolen goods. Thus it was that the Dalton Gang turned to the high-stakes business of robbing trains.

Bob, Emmett, "Blackface" Charley Bryant and "Bitter Creek" Newcomb held up their first train at Wharton (modern-day Perry) in Oklahoma Territory in May 1891. They escaped with $1700. The ease with which the gang pulled off the robbery and the quantity of cash nabbed, combined with a long-standing hatred of the railroad companies, encouraged the Daltons to continue in their newfound calling.

Following the Wharton robbery, "Blackface" Charley Bryant became ill. While at a doctor's office in Hennessey, Oklahoma Territory, he was arrested by Marshal Ed Short. Short was a sworn enemy of the Daltons and one of the determined lawmen who had been dogging the gang for months. He had been biding his time for the most part, waiting for the evidence solid enough to break up the gang and put its members behind bars for good. But while transporting Bryant by train to a federal jail in Wichita, Short failed to prevent the outlaw from getting his hands on a gun; Bryant's desperate bid to escape led to a shoot-out that left both men dead.

The Dalton Gang struck again at Lelietta on September 15, 1891. The job netted them $2500. Shortly thereafter, Grat surprised the gang members by suddenly resurfacing in Oklahoma Territory. He had busted out of the jail in Visalia by sawing through the bars and had ridden all the way back east to rejoin his brothers.

The Daltons next robbed the Red Rock depot on June 1, 1892. The first train to pull into the depot had its windows darkened; on the order of Bob Dalton, the bandits stayed put. It was a wise decision. The train carried not only a large sum of cash, but also a company of well-armed lawmen who intended to surprise the train robbers with a show of considerable firepower. The second train held little in the way of resistance, but yielded a mere $50 for the bandits. The Dalton Gang would hold up only one more train before opting for bigger stakes.

On July 14, 1892, the moon was a sliver behind wispy clouds. A light wind skipped across the dark plains near the depot at Adair in Oklahoma Territory. The members of the Dalton Gang huddled their horses together.

Bob Dalton rehearsed the plans for the robbery again. He went over the positions he wanted each man to assume, and, having made his strategy clear, lit a cheroot for himself. The brief flare illuminated his rocky features. He turned his horse and rode down the track a little way. Emmett watched his shadow fade away into the blackness and shifted uneasily in his saddle. Grat Dalton scowled and raised a flask to his lips. Powers joked softly with Broadwell and Newcomb, but they did not laugh and his voice died back down into silence. The horses stamped their hooves with impatience. They all waited for the lonesome sound of the train whistle.

The gang had rigged the signal light to show red, which meant "problems up ahead on the tracks." Grat had taken out the lone telegraph clerk with a crack to the head from the butt of his pistol. He had been ready to put a bullet through the young man's brain, but Bob had rebuked him sharply.

"There's no need for that Grat. He's just a kid, working for the damn railroad. You'll get your chance to fire that thing. Now go and take your place."

Now Grat waited as Bob had said. The night was quiet. He swallowed the last of his whiskey, wiped his mouth with the sleeve of his greatcoat, and tossed the empty bottle over his shoulder. And then, far off in the distance, he heard the sound of the engine.

Acknowledging the glowing red light, the locomotive slowly decelerated and ground to a shuddering halt. Anxious passengers looked out into the dark night. Some men hefted their purses into their pockets, while others cocked their revolvers and peered out into the inky darkness.

Suddenly, the train was invaded by bandits. The Dalton Gang swarmed into the cars and subdued the terrified passengers. Grat, Emmett, and the others swaggered down the aisle, randomly firing shots into the roof to hasten the surrender of purses and valuables. Bob and Dick Broadwell burst into the locomotive, causing the fireman and brakeman to yelp with terror. The badmen had reared out of the gloom like phantoms.

"Open the safe!" snarled Bob Dalton. Broadwell menaced the cowering fireman with his pistol.

Within 10 minutes, the gang had scooped up all that was to be had, including a considerable stack of banknotes. As they were departing, however, a contingent of railroad guards arrived at the scene of the crime and engaged the gang in gunfire.

Bullets ricocheted off the metal coaches as the Daltons scrambled to their mounts. A number of men from both sides were wounded in the crossfire, and a local doctor who had arrived with the railroad guards was killed by a shot through the eye. The chief of the railroad guards and the leader of the Cherokee Nation police force were also wounded in the gunfight. Somehow, the gang of outlaws escaped.

It could not be proven whose bullet had caused the death of the good doctor. Nevertheless, because the Daltons were crack shots, the townspeople and lawmen alike immediately blamed the notorious bandits. They were enraged by the senseless death and appalled at the seeming impunity with which the desperadoes operated.

The robbery at Adair caused the forces of the law to redouble their efforts to catch the thieves. They called in Pinkerton detectives to end the Daltons' crime streak. Ultimately, increased security on the railroads prompted the gang to shift its attention to banks. This decision marked the beginning of the path that would end on a cool fall afternoon in Coffeyville, Kansas, on a little side-street that would come to bear the name "Death Alley."

Bob was astute enough to take the gun battle at Adair as a sign of things to come. He decided it was once more time for a change. Besides, he was growing more than a little tired of the life of the fugitive. Even when holed up in the safest of hideouts, he couldn't be sure that some glory seeker wouldn't suddenly burst in on him with pistols blazing. Most of the gang members had gone their separate ways after the train robbery at Adair, so when Bob proposed robbing both the Condon Bank and the First National in the brothers' hometown of Coffeyville, he did so to a smaller group than usual. The daring feat would ensure the gang's place in the annals of history. What's more, the huge windfall would earn them a reprieve from their hectic routine of continual crime.

Bob emphasized the first point when he unveiled the plan to Grat, Emmett, Powers and Broadwell. Wealth and fame beckoned. Here was a chance to do something no one else had done. "Our names will go down in history," Bob said as he explained his plan for hitting both banks simultaneously. "Emmett and I will deal with the First National. Grat, Bill and Dick will hit the Condon. We'll meet back at the horses in no more than five minutes—and gallop off to freedom and the good life!"

Grat Dalton just grunted and turned away, leaving the others hunched over Bob's stick-drawings in the sand. Grat wanted nothing more than to get money and drink it away. Bob was a pain and Emmett was still wet behind the ears. Neither of them knew what it was like to be in jail, or to ride across half a continent alone. Powers and Broadwell meant nothing to him.

On October 5, 1892, the five principal members of the Dalton Gang rode out from their camp near Onion Creek toward Coffeyville. They had pulled their hats low and donned fake beards and mustaches. The morning was cool but pleasant, and the sun warmed their backs. Through fields of harvest and along dusty roads lined with corn they wound their way. A number of citizens of Coffeyville passed them but failed to recognize the famous outlaw gang. It was assumed that they were deputy marshals, or part of a special posse. Slouched low in their saddles, they rode slowly into Coffeyville. Three rode in front, two behind. The moment of truth was at hand, in the town of their youth.

The two banks were located directly across from one another. The first thing the Daltons realized was that they could not hitch their horses by the opera house as planned—workmen were replacing cobblestones there. They spurred their horses on to a secluded spot in the alley, where they dismounted and secured the animals. The more ornate and solid Condon was now the closer bank. Grat, Powers and Broadwell, each carrying a Winchester, led the way up the alley and barged into the Condon Bank. It was 9:15 AM.

Bob Dalton and his younger brother Emmett pulled their bandannas over their faces and stormed into the First National. "Open the safe and do it quickly," snarled Bob, as Emmett threatened the tellers and two customers with his rifle.

"For goodness' sake, Bob! Emmett!" said one of the townsfolk, recognizing them through their disguises. "What the hell are you boys up to now?"

A passer-by glanced into the bank and saw Emmett Dalton in his blue bandanna, leveling his rifle at another man. "The Daltons are robbing the bank!" he cried, scurrying for safety. Despite being completely caught off guard—there was not a single armed guard in the vicinity of the banks when the Daltons began their holdup—the townspeople quickly brought in teams of horses to block off the streets. They pried open a crate of repeater rifles, which had been shipped by lawmen the previous week, and passed out the weapons to anyone with enough courage and fortitude to take on the renowned Dalton Gang.

Headquartered at the Isham and Mansur Hardware Store, which adjoined the First National Bank, the brave citizens of Coffeyville had a clear view of the Condon Bank across the street. They loaded their rifles and began to fire at the shadowy figures inside the bank.

Inside, bank clerk Charles Ball was explaining to Grat Dalton that the safe was locked with a timer and wouldn't open for another 15 minutes. He was lying. The safe had sprung open promptly at 8:30 AM, but Grat was fooled.

"We'll wait," he declared, even as bullets began to strike the walls and shatter the windows.

Powers shot out a window and slouched into position under its frame; his rifle began to seek out the citizens who were shooting from the other side of the street. Dick Broadwell similarly entrenched himself in the opposite corner.

At the First National, Bob was stuffing money into a cloth sack and cursing the decision to have Grat and the others pull off the Condon part of the heist. Marching the clerk, W.H. Shepard, in front of him, Bob handed the loot to Emmett and exited the bank by its rear door—only to be greeted by the whine of more bullets and a haze of blue gun smoke.

Coolly selecting targets across the street despite the thick dust, Bob wheeled and fired; his bullet smashed both the gunstock and the hand of one Charlie Gump. A second, long-range shot killed Lucius Baldwin dead, and an eerie pause hung momentarily over the battle. Most of the citizens were still waiting for Bob and Emmett to emerge from the front door of the First National. George B. Cubine was one of those waiting. As the outlaws rounded the building, they spied Cubine waiting in the doorway of the drug store. Bob surprised him with a bullet to the heart. Thomas Ayres also fell victim to the wicked accuracy of Bob's Winchester.

At the same time, Grat Dalton, Powers and Broadwell stumbled from the Condon Bank and retreated to the alley. A heavy bag weighed Powers down, and blood streamed from Broadwell's useless, bullet-shredded arm. Grat covered his fellow desperadoes and blazed away at the advancing townspeople until a bullet rocked him backwards. He thumped to the ground. Blood stained the front of his shirt.

Powers, too, was hit several times in the murderous crossfire. It was apparent that the gang members would be lucky to escape with their lives, let alone the money. Their dreams of living out a life in South America or Mexico, unencumbered by vigilantes and lawmen, were fading in the harsh light of reality.

Trapped in Death Alley by seemingly ubiquitous gunmen, the Dalton Gang struggled to reach the horses. Bob Dalton had just released his hostage when he was struck by two bullets. He lurched back toward the small barn in the alley, spitting blood. In desperation, he advanced against the citizenry of Coffeyville in a last, lethal charge. Chaos erupted from the business end of his gun.

Powers was shot dead, and Grat Dalton was hit several more times before a final, close-range shot from the rifle of John Kloehr finished him off.

Dick Broadwell made it up onto his horse. The crazed animal raced away from the smoky confusion of the gun battle, but its rider was dying even as it galloped out of town. Broadwell was thrown from the saddle dead less than an eighth of a mile outside of Coffeyville.

Emmett also made it to his horse, but was hit several times in doing so. Although he still clutched the sack of money from the First National, he was badly wounded and focused only on his adored older brother, Bob, who was slowly dying in the dusty street. Emmett reached down to Bob through the haze.

But the leader of the Dalton Gang had fallen. "Emmett," he gasped. Bob's breast was slick and shiny; the dark blood reflected the morning sunlight. "Save yourself," he whispered, even as Emmett tried desperately to pull him up onto the horse. The warning came too late. Carey Seamen emptied the contents of his double-barreled shotgun into the youngest Dalton's back. The force sent Emmett crashing to the ground.

Less than 15 minutes had passed since the first shot was fired. The alley was a gruesome display of carnage. Of the gang members, only Emmett was still alive—and even he was bleeding heavily from a shotgun blast to the back. Three citizens were mortally wounded. Stillness hung in the air for a moment. "They're all down!" cried one of the town's defenders, prompting the rest of the men to lower their guns and descend on the decimated Dalton gang.

The dead bandits were handcuffed and propped up for immortality by photographer John Tackett, and then stretched out in a row like so much firewood. Talk of lynching the surviving Dalton was dispelled and Emmett was hustled off to have his wounds tended by a surgeon. He would survive; in a brief moment of clarity, he insisted that his arm not be cut off, despite being told that amputation was the only way to save his life.

Emmett Dalton was sentenced to life in prison for his part in the fatal raid that claimed the lives of his brothers and fellow conspirators. Paroled in 1907 by the governor of Kansas, he became a celebrity and a wealthy contractor in California. He married his boyhood sweetheart and made a great deal of money recounting his tales of "outlawdom" in books and movies. He died a "model citizen" in 1937.

The elimination of Bob and Grat by the citizens of Coffeyville on that warm October morning in 1892 was not the end of the Dalton Gang. After burying his brothers, Bill Dalton hooked up with Bill Doolin and other gang members who had not been in Coffeyville on that fateful day, and the newly named Doolin-Dalton Gang went back to pulling off train robberies.

The lawlessness of the territories was waning, however, and the desperate outlaws were relentlessly pursued. One by one, the members were either captured or killed. Bill Dalton was shot to death near his farm and his body displayed in a glass-covered coffin. Children and adults alike paid a nickel to view the remains of the last of the fearsome Dalton Gang until the body had completely decomposed. Bill Doolin was hunted down in a cave and riddled with lead; in death, he looked as though he were covered in pennies. His eyes stood open, wide and staring, as if he were finally seeing the answer to a question that had stumped him for a long time.

SAM BASS, AGED 16

9

Sam Bass

Sam Bass was born in Indiana, it was his native home;
And at the age of 17 young Sam began to roam.
Sam first came out to Texas, a cowboy for to be—
A kinder-hearted fellow you seldom ever see.

Not long after Sam Bass's death in 1878, these lines were sung all along the range, from Texas to Wyoming. As herds of longhorns settled down after a hard dusty day, you could hear cowboys crooning "The Ballad of Sam Bass" into the lonely prairie wind, eulogizing the life of a likable young outlaw whose days were so violently cut short by the fierce justice of the West. Yet Sam Bass was not, to use his own words, "born to robbing"; he just drifted into outlawry like a tumbleweed into a split-rail fence.

Born near Mitchell, Indiana on July 21, 1851, Bass spent most of his life toiling as a homesteader. His parents died when he was young, leaving Sam in the care of his uncle Dave Seeks, a stern Christian moralist who held nothing above the virtue of a hard day's work. Sam's relationship with his severe uncle became strained as he grew older; gambling trips to nearby Juliet, coupled with mounting arguments over proper pay, took their toll on the peace in the Seeks household. Though Sam was a hard worker, his sense of adventure seemed to demand more than life on the homestead could offer. Finally, on a fall evening in 1869, fueled by dreams of being a cowboy and hopes that reached beyond the limits of his uncle's farm, the young Hoosier ran away from home with nothing but the clothes on his back.

A year later, Sam drifted into Denton, Texas with a horse, saddle and six-shooter at his side—a wiser, if somewhat jaded young man. Over the past year, he had spent more than six months in Rosedale, Mississippi, laboring in a sawmill, sweating his days away to earn the basic gear of a cowhand. As soon as he had bought the equipment, Sam headed straight for Texas, cattle country, to realize his dream of life on the range. He found work on a ranch near Denton, but after his first winter and spring of work, Sam's romantic notions of life as a cowboy had been dispelled. It turned out life on the ranch offered labor that was just as grueling, isolated and monotonous as on the homestead. So it was that a disillusioned Sam Bass rode into Denton in the fall of 1870 hoping to find different work in a more sociable environment.

It is one of the more ironic turns in the history of the West that Sam found work as a hired hand and teamster for Sheriff W.F. "Dad" Eagan, probably the most famous lawman of Denton County. Furthermore, Sam so distinguished himself as an honest and diligent worker that he was given the nickname "Honest Eph," which would stick with the young bandit even as he was being chased across Texas by half the lawmen of the state. The road that led Sam from being an upstanding citizen to a wanted bandit was a short one.

Throughout his life, Sam exhibited a weakness for gambling. As a teenager in Indiana, Sam's gambling habit was the root of the biggest rows with his uncle. While Sam was working in Rosedale, he relied on card games at the local saloon to ease the dull routine of his exhausting work at the mill. In Denton the same need for excitement drove him to the horse races; yet the difference in Denton was Sam's remarkable success. For the first time, it appeared Lady Luck was smiling on Sam Bass.

In the fall of 1874, he bought Jenny, a chestnut-sorrel mare that grew to be the fastest horse in town. Before long, Jenny was taking on contenders from other locales, and getting Sam into dodgy situations with dubious characters. Eagan was not happy about Sam's link to the shady gambling world, especially since Eagan's own association with Sam compromised the sheriff's reputation as a lawman. During spring of the following year, "Dad" Eagan gave Sam an ultimatum: lose Jenny or lose the job. Given that Sam had worked like a mule all of his life and had almost nothing to show for it, the young man's decision to go with his mare, which continued to gallop ahead with a string of victories, wasn't too surprising. So Sam quit working for Eagan, and lived life in the fast track for a short while: traveling to different towns, winning big and spending just as much. Sam earned a reputation as a genuine *bon vivant*, regularly frequenting saloons, playing cards, enjoying the best cigars and drinking fine whiskey.

It was at this time that Sam met the infamous cowboy and saloonkeeper Joel Collins, the man who would lead Sam into a life of crime. Accounts differ as to how depraved a man Collins was, for though it was well known that he had shot a man in southern Texas, he was lawfully acquitted by a State jury. Regardless, when Sam Bass met Collins in 1875 in San Antonio, he was no saint either. Resorting to fixing races to keep the winnings coming in, Bass's corrupt practices had attracted Collins to him, and the two began scamming everyone they could from San Antonio to the Rio Grande. Before long, they became known among gamesters as confidence men, and their careers in horse racing were suddenly over. Having dried up their prospects at the racetrack, their extravagant lifestyles were quickly consuming what savings they had, and soon Bass was almost as poor as he was when he had arrived in Texas five years earlier.

Collins, though, was not the type of man given to panic, and in August of 1876 he devised a plan that would send the two friends up the cattle trail to Kansas with a herd of nearly 500 steers. They had a little money, and Collins had connections with ranchers in southwest Texas, so they were able to secure trust for the delivery of the cattle. Upon hiring a few extra cowhands, the intrepid pair began the long drive up to Kansas. It turned out to be a profitable venture, for when they sold the cattle in northwest Kansas, Collins and Bass were able to pay off the hired hands and still walk away with $8000 between them. Of course most of the money belonged to the Texan ranchers who had sold them the steers, but the two friends were far too elated with their sudden fortune to return it. Instead of riding back to Texas, the pair headed north up to the Black Hills in the dangerous Dakota Territory where speculators were mining for gold. In the violent mining town of Deadwood, Sam's dissolute tendencies would be nourished by chaotic surroundings.

Deadwood was the same town where Wild Bill Hickok had met his end in 1871, a bullet shot into his back during a poker game; it was a lawless town that seemed to have more saloons than houses, and depended upon the patronage of gold miners for its survival. A town devoid of the genteel influences of proper society, it was the perfect place for Sam's complete slide into vice.

Collins and Bass soon squandered away all of their money on cards, whiskey and women; and so with the help of four other rogues—Bill Hefferidge, Jim Berry, Tom Nixon and Jack Davis—they took to stagecoach robbing to get them through the harsh winter of 1877. Bass's first experiences with robbery at gunpoint were certainly not auspicious. In late March, one of the men accidentally shot a stagecoach driver through the chest when a horse got spooked and bolted in the middle of a robbery. The slain teamster was a popular man, and his death brought the ire of the community down upon the gang. By the summer of 1877, the group was still broke, and their latest haul consisted of one passenger's $6. With their last heist in late August, Collins, Bass and the bandits had robbed seven stages in total, and all together had only about $100 to show for it. The desperate men were also facing increasing vigilante pressure as the number of their robberies mounted. The situation got so bad that in September of 1877 that the bandits turned their backs on Deadwood for good, riding south into Nebraska with next to nothing in their saddlebags.

Once again, Joel Collins had a plan.

Outlaws had been holding up trains ever since the Reno Brothers led the first gang of organized train robbers in 1866. Legend had it that the brothers once hauled in $90,000 in a single heist near Seymour, Indiana. While Collins, Bass and the gang had miserable luck robbing coaches in Dakota, they certainly were not about to become honest men, so it was almost natural that Collins' ravenous eye turned to another sort of hijacking: train robbery. Sure enough, stopping and boarding a full train was an entirely different business than robbing a stagecoach; but Collins had faith in his gang of seasoned, if destitute, bandits. Thus, with the confident deliberation that was characteristic of him, Collins orchestrated the hold-up of the Union Pacific train in Big Springs, Nebraska. This robbery was the one that put the gang down in history.

There was a bright moon out on the night of September 18, illuminating the water-station at Big Springs as the bandits took position around it. At 10:48, they overwhelmed the stationmaster, forcing him to light a red lantern to stop the approaching express train. Before it had come to a full stop, Collins and Hefferidge stormed aboard the locomotive, capturing the engineer and the fireman with cocked revolvers.

In the meantime, Bass and Davis went after the loot. They quickly apprehended the express messenger, a man named Charley Miller, and broke into the way-safe, nabbing $450. Complications arose when they spotted the large iron through-safe. Miller was unable to open the compartment because it had been set on a timer in San Francisco, triggered to open upon arrival in Omaha. With a trembling voice Miller explained that he did not know the combination: "Gentlemen, I give you my word of honor I don't know it. You may kill me if you want to, but I tell you honestly I don't know it."

Miller showed Bass and Davis official papers that backed his story, but neither of the men could read. Davis thought the messenger was bluffing and broke into a nasty rage, giving the poor man an awful beating with his pistol. By the time Collins had arrived to check the men's progress, Charley Miller was hurt badly, his face bleeding heavily and two or three of his teeth missing. Upon reading the messenger's documents, Collins verified Miller's story and ordered Davis to let him be. In desperation, Sam seized an axe and tried to smash the safe open, but his efforts were in vain. The Union Pacific had taken every precaution with the transportation of this particular cargo, for the safe contained $200,000 in gold.

All was not lost. As the three men ransacked the express car they stumbled across three small wooden boxes that were sealed in wax. Davis axed one of the boxes open whereupon, amidst a sudden silence, $20 gold pieces spilled across the floor. Each box contained no less than $20,000 in gold, amounting to a take of $60,000 in the three boxes. Though this moment was most definitely the greatest of the bandits' criminal careers, all records show they maintained their poise.

The six colleagues efficiently finished the job. While Berry and Nixon stood guard on the platform, Hefferidge and Collins watched over the doors of the coaches as Bass and Davis robbed the passengers. The menacing Jack Davis would storm into each compartment, taking the passengers' cash and jewelry. "Hold up your hands and keep still!" Davis hollered, six-shooter in hand. "We want your money."

Here Sam demonstrated his peculiar sort of kindness. As he made his way through one coach, he noticed an elderly gentleman with only one arm. "Take back your stuff," said Sam, "we don't want your money. Sit down and keep still."

They acquired about another $400 from the passengers in the coaches before they disappeared north into the Nebraska night.

Who knows what Sam was thinking as he sped away with his friends that evening? After the Big Springs holdup he was richer than he probably ever thought he would be. Also, unlike the thousands of other Westerners who toiled on their farms, on their ranches, in their shops or in the mines, Sam had made his fortune in a matter of minutes. Perhaps it was during this evening, in the wake of such an astounding success contrasted to his many years of honest—though fruitless—labor, that Sam Bass finally defined himself. Maybe it was on this night that Sam Bass crystallized into a *bona fide* outlaw. What is certain is that from that night on, Sam Bass never again even considered the idea of making an honest living.

After the robbery, the gang split into three groups of two so as to avoid suspicion. Bass and Collins said their farewells just outside of Ogallala, Nebraska. Sam went back to Denton with Jack Davis, while Joel Collins and Bill Hefferidge headed down to San Antonio. Jim Berry and Tom Nixon set their sights east for Missouri. Within a day of the robbery, however, Nebraska and Kansas were crawling with posses motivated by the Union Pacific prompt reward of $10,000 for each of the brigands. Collins and Hefferidge were gunned down not a week after the heist as they tried to escape from an Ellis County sheriff and his posse who were hot on their trail. In Missouri, a lawman shot Berry dead on October 14. Nixon went up north to Canada, never to be heard from again.

Of the three groups, only Bass and Davis made it safely to their destination. Trading one of their horses for a buggy as soon as possible, they posed as impoverished farmers from western Kansas as they proceeded south. On one night, they even camped out with a squad of soldiers who were hunting for them, $20,000 in gold coins hidden in the bottom of their old buggy. This is the first record of Sam's talent at eluding authorities; it was precisely this ability, his knack at pulling off such daring escapes, that would make Sam Bass a folk hero.

Sam and Jack Davis arrived in Denton on November 1, 1877. Shortly afterwards Davis took a train south to New Orleans and, like Tom Nixon, disappeared into anonymity. It seems that Sam barely paused at all to consider the disintegration of the Big Springs gang. Now that he was back in Denton, a rich man surrounded by old friends, he continued to live the only way he knew how. Jovial old "Honest Eph" explained his obvious wealth by telling people he had made a fortune in the Black Hills as a gold speculator. Thus Sam resumed his life in Denton, living even more exorbitantly than he did three years previous when no horse in northern Texas could best Jenny on the racetrack. His old gambling friends, Frank Jackson, Henry Underwood and Henderson Murphy, practically became his disciples, held in awe at the apparently bottomless depths of his wallet. Sam was certainly generous with his money, buying for his friends wherever he went. Many of the people in Denton County, especially squatters in the surrounding countryside, took personal joy in the success story of the amiable young drifter who wandered into their town seven years ago. Sam would test these friendships before long.

It is unclear if Sam began plotting theft again because he was running out of money, or because his unruly nature began to get the better of him. Surely the public excitement caused by the train robbery at Allen Station on December 20, the first train robbery in northern Texas, must have stirred his blood. Yet either way, not a year after his arrival in Denton, Sam began scheming. He planned to hold up a train with his own gang, confident in his ability to lead after his experience at Big Springs.

He first confided in Jackson, Underwood and Murphy about the real origin of his wealth. His friends were impressed, and with the exception of Henderson Murphy, who was too old for Bass's tomfoolery, it did not take much convincing to get them to join up for the adventures that Sam was promising.

Meanwhile, Sheriff Eagan, who was suspicious of Sam's return from the onset, had quickly connected the young man's sudden fortune to the robbery at Big Springs. Denton suddenly grew more dangerous as Eagan began a manhunt for Sam. In response, Bass's gang quickly established a hideout. The band made camp in Cove Hollow, an almost inaccessible part of the canyon that flanked Clear Creek. While Henderson Murphy's house fronted the only feasible path into the copse, the wood was so overgrown with thick brush and teeming with rattlesnakes that very few people ventured into it. Yet the bandits would still suffer an early setback when Henry Underwood left Cove Hollow to visit his family home on Christmas Eve that year. In a bizarre case of mistaken identity he was locked up in a Nebraska prison on the pretext that he was Tom Nixon, Sam's old friend who had disappeared in Canada after the Big Springs robbery.

Undeterred by the sudden loss of one of their own and the increasing attention of the law, Bass's foolhardy gang carried out its first holdup in Hutchins, on the night of March 18, 1878. There were only three robbers that evening: Sam, Frank Jackson and Seaborn Barnes, a rough new recruit who was known all across Denton County for his viciousness. Compared to the Big Springs robbery, Hutchins was anything but a success. This time, the express messenger engaged the bandits in short-lived gunfire but was soon overcome. Sam and his band only nabbed about $3000, missing the large sum of money that the same brave railway employee had hidden in the stove before the fight.

The next three train robberies that the band committed over the following month were even less successful. While the take of the subsequent robberies never equaled the $3000 at Hutchins, Bass's men were facing mounting resistance from the train employees. During the last robbery at Mesquite on April 10, 1878, Barnes received four minor wounds when a gunfight ensued with the conductor. Though the band had not lost anyone yet, their enthusiasm for train robbery waned as the expeditions grew ever more violent and less profitable. Nevertheless, Bass was always looking ahead to the next heist, vainly trying to relive the glory of the Big Springs success.

However, the law in Texas had different plans for Bass. While Sheriff Eagan was hunting down Sam for the Union Pacific holdup in Nebraska, the public protest at the sudden number of train robberies in northern Texas was brought to Governor R.B. Hubbard's attention. The governor acted quickly, and by the end of April, 50 Texas Rangers under Captain June Peak were commissioned to bring the perpetrators of the Texas robberies to justice. Peak had been studying the crimes even before he was officially commissioned, and was convinced that the Texas robbers were the same brigands that Eagan's posse was looking for. Thus the dreadful weight of the Texas Rangers was added to the Denton posses, and young Sam Bass would soon be in for the rush of his life.

So began what the local newspapers called "The Bass War," a mad hunt for Bass's gang that sent the hunters and hunted across half of Texas over a period of three months. It was during this period that Sam would almost joyfully lead his band from one daring escape to another. "The Bass War" pitted about five men against over 200; it would be Sam's willingness to gamble against these impossible odds that would make him into a legend.

The first shots of the war were fired when Peak's and Eagan's lawmen plunged into the thicket of Cove Hollow on April 25, 1878 intent on flushing the bandits out quickly. Sam must have been in an especially jovial mood, because Underwood had just recently rejoined the band after having escaped from prison in Nebraska. In addition, he brought with him "Arkansaw" Johnson, a cold-blooded man who was reputed never to lose his calm in a gunfight. As the woods filled with armed lawmen bent on the death or capture of the outlaws, Johnson advised Bass that against such odds it would be best to cut out fast and head straight for Mexico. The panicked crew must have liked the sound of Johnson's reasoning, but Sam would have no part of it. Reveling in the gamble, he was determined to remain in Cove Hollow as long as he could. It is a statement either to Sam's personal magnetism, or the loyalty of his friends, that they stuck by him.

As the ring of men closed around the band's camp, they came out of hiding, hitting the contingent of lawmen under Eagan's command. Under the cover of heavy forest, the bandits broke free of the firing as the numerous posses disintegrated into confusion at the sound of battle. Lack of proper leadership was one of the biggest difficulties the lawmen faced in apprehending Sam's gang. Because the Union Pacific reward was still on Sam's head, competing posses were vying for Sam's capture, making each group eager to claim the reward money for themselves. So the hunters fell into a confused mob, with Eagan's group firing on another sheriff's men, and Peak's Rangers stumbling bewildered out of the copse. Miraculously, no one was hurt.

Sam must have whooped for joy as his gang left the baffled lawmen behind them, navigating the dense wood to arrive at Henderson Murphy's home. Four days later, the lawmen hit again, a group of them spotting the men at Murphy's

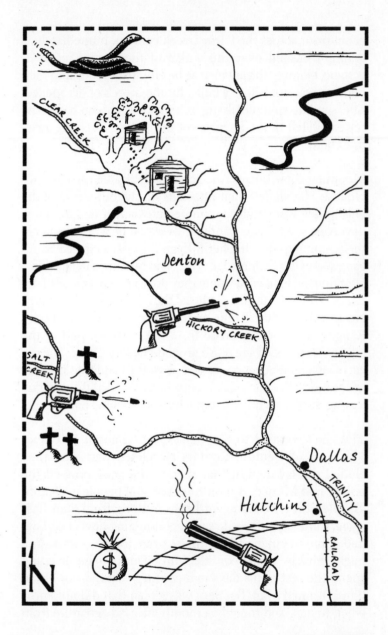

NORTHERN TEXAS

cabin from across the Clear Creek canyon. Immediately, a gunfight ensued over the width of the gorge. Sam was ecstatic, taunting the lawmen as he emptied rounds into their midst. It was not before a bullet hit the breech of his Spencer rifle, sending splinters flying in his face, that Sam called the retreat: "Hell boys! They've hit me at last. Let's get away from here!"

Mounting their horses, the robbers finally fled from Cove Hollow. Having left their attackers on the other side of the gulch, they were under no immediate danger and for a few days rode south quite calmly. This would be a rare respite in the upcoming month. Sheriff Eagan's posse engaged Sam's gang soon after their escape. The band became entangled in a tight running fight all day until they dove into cover in Hickory Creek. This time Eagan marshaled the full might of the county. No less than 150 citizens under Eagan, along with Peak's Rangers and another posse from the northern part of the county, surrounded the brush around Hickory Creek. The circle of lawmen once more closed in on the bandits as they lay concealed in the thicket, and once more Sam led the way out, leaving the posses firing into the darkness behind him.

The band escaped to Stephens County, about 100 miles southeast of Denton. Rumors circulated that after they eluded the lawmen of that region, the gang crossed the border into Mexico. A month passed, and people in Denton assumed they would never hear anything from Sam Bass again. Certainly this made sense, considering how close Sam had come to paying the ultimate price for his crimes. You might think he would consider himself lucky to be alive, and spend the rest of his days in a country that did not brand him a Wanted Man. But Sam was a man that did not know when to quit, and roughly a month after his departure from

Sheriff Eagan's county, he came back and pulled the craziest stunt of his life.

On June 6 at about six o'clock in the morning, Sam and his gang came tearing down Main Street into the heart of Denton. They had come to take back two horses they had lost when they escaped from Hickory Creek about a month earlier. As Bass and Jackson dashed into Work's livery stable, Barnes, Johnson and Underwood remained at the door, revolvers drawn. After Jackson had soundly beaten the stableman, the horses were secured and the gang was off. As the reckless band galloped away, Underwood woke the sleeping town with a hearty laugh, shouting, "Damn 'em, we'll show 'em they can't steal anything from us that we can't get back!" Shortly after, when the beaten stableman and the two missing horses were discovered, the town became a hornet's nest. As quickly as could be managed, Sheriff Eagan had a posse together and was giving full chase.

Eagan was angry now. This boy that he had taken into his home as a hired hand eight years ago had made him look like a fool too many times. He urged his posse into a frantic pursuit. The sheriff stopped at nothing, giving Sam's gang no time to rest. For three days, the law was just a breath behind the bandits, cornering them into two full-out gun battles that the outlaws only escaped from by the skin of their teeth. The gang was so hard pressed over those three days that the characteristically good humor among them all but vanished. They scarcely had a chance to eat or sleep, and the mood was desperate by the time Sam's gang ducked into Salt Creek bottom on June 8.

Late in the afternoon of that day, as Sam's tired band was preparing to make camp near the bank of Salt Creek, Peak's Rangers practically stumbled into them—the two parties were mere yards away from each other. The first to react on either side was Underwood, who bolted for the horses that were staked nearby. Not a second later, weapons were drawn and a fierce gunfight ensued. "Arkansaw" Johnson lived up to his reputation, calmly covering the rapid retreat of his colleagues by emptying his Winchester rifle and revolver into the ranks of the Rangers. Yet before he could turn to find better cover, he took a single bullet straight in the chest and died where he stood. By this time the rest of the gang had found a shallow cave in the creek bank, and prayed for night to come quickly. They were all there except Underwood, who had led the horses into the woods; he was mounted and anxiously waiting, wondering which of his friends would emerge to make the getaway. Instead, he was greeted by Captain Peak himself, who immediately opened fire. After a short exchange of rounds, Underwood put spurs to his horse and tore out of the copse. He was never heard from again.

When night fell, Bass, Jackson and Barnes furtively made their way out of Salt Creek; under cover of darkness, they began their weary hike back to Cove Hollow. The noose was quickly tightening, however, for Peak's sharp police work during Bass's long absence from Denton County compromised the security of the band's old hideout. Henderson Murphy's son Jim was a rat.

During the month of May, Peak had quickly arrested anyone who was suspected of harboring Sam Bass during his crime spree. Among the many citizens who were caught in this dragnet were Henderson and Jim Murphy, the residents of the old cabin at Cove Hollow. Under threats of imprisonment aimed at him and his father, Jim Murphy cracked. He agreed to act undercover, and inform the law of the whereabouts of Bass's next heist as soon as he was able. It was June 15 when Bass and Jackson made it back from the debacle at

Salt Creek. Still intent on robbery and short of manpower, Bass recruited Murphy into his band. The trap was set. The trio rode out to meet with Barnes who had split up with Bass and Jackson on the way back from Salt Creek.

The plan was almost blown twice. First, Murphy almost panicked when the trio met up with Barnes, who had gotten wind of a botched telegram that revealed Murphy's role in the plot. Barnes was going to shoot Murphy himself, but was talked out of it by Jackson, who vouched for Murphy: "I've known Jim for a long time. I know he won't give me away, nor you either."

As the memory of Salt Creek began to fade and the band's mood lightened, they began to give serious thought to their next heist. Here, for the second time, Murphy was overcome by panic. When the gang wandered into Waco, they noted that robbing the bank there straight away would be ideal. If they did go through with it, the traitor would not have been able to get word out to the authorities. Murphy implored the men not to rob the bank in every way he knew how. The next morning, Bass suddenly deferred to Murphy's pleas, and called the robbery off, somehow convinced by Murphy's warnings: "Well, Jim, if you think there is too much danger here at Waco, we will not hit it. We will go wherever you say."

On Sunday, July 13 Murphy sent a telegram to Sheriff Everheart of Grayson County and Deputy U.S. Marshal Walter Johnson, telling them that a bank robbery was to take place in Round Rock later that week. As the gang staked out the town on July 15, Murphy was able to get a more detailed message away, warning the lawmen to be ready for a robbery on Saturday July 20, at 3:30 PM. Events, however, did not go exactly as planned.

The four men rode into Round Rock on Friday afternoon to purchase some tobacco. The town was already filling up with Rangers, and perhaps Murphy could sense trouble coming. He told his companions he would wait on the outskirts of town. According to legend, Bass and Jackson were careful enough to keep their revolvers in their saddlebags when they rode into town, but Barnes kept his holstered on his belt. As they walked into Henry Kopel's tobacco store, a draft caught Barnes' riding jacket and revealed his firearm underneath. Deputy Sheriff Moore noticed this, and almost casually mentioned it Deputy Sheriff Grimes.

The two lawmen walked into Kopel's shop, where the ill-fated Grimes carelessly asked any of the men if they were carrying pistols. Reportedly, all three men turned and answered, "Yes," whereupon the bandits drew their pistols and shot the deputy sheriff dead. Moore instantly returned fire, but he did not have a clear line of sight for all the smoke that was suddenly in the room. As he was hit once in the chest, Moore emptied five rounds into the room, blowing Bass's middle fingers off his pistol hand. As the three men lurched outside, Rangers came flooding out of the surrounding buildings, drawn by the sound of gunfire. Within minutes, bullets were cutting through the air around them. The three men returned fire while tearing down the alley to where their horses were tethered. Seaborn Barnes was stopped midstride, shot through the back of the head. He died instantly. Just before they got to their steeds, Sam took a bullet in the gut and collapsed against his horse's flank as he tried to mount. In critical seconds, Jackson ran through the stream of bullets that washed over them, and helped his friend up into the saddle.

Somehow, with Frank Jackson holding Sam up on his horse, the men managed to make it out of Round Rock. They tore past the crowd of Rangers as the lawmen closed in with guns blazing. But Sam knew that his luck had run out. A couple miles out of town, the mortally wounded outlaw was too weak to continue, and insisted that Jackson leave him and save himself. Painfully propping himself up against an oak tree, Bass sat through the night and waited for the inevitable. He was still alive when a search party discovered him the next day.

"Don't shoot; I am helpless," he croaked weakly. "I am the man you are looking for. I am Sam Bass."

Bass was promptly interrogated by the highest-ranking officer in Round Rock, Major John B. Jones of the Texas Rangers. Jones would later state: "I tried every conceivable plan to obtain some information from him, but to no purpose."

By noon Sunday, Sam's condition grew worse, and it was obvious he was about to die. Jones made a final effort to get some clues as to the whereabouts of Frank Jackson, yet once again, he was rebuffed. When Jones asked for an explanation for Sam's stubbornness, even in the face of death, the bandit replied, "Because it is ag'in my profession to blow on my pals. If a man knows anything he ought to die with it in him."

Not much else was said between the two. At one point, Sam stated that from the outset of his criminal career, he never intended to hurt anyone, and that if he had been the one who killed Deputy Grimes, it was the first man he had slain.

Finally, at 3:58 on Sunday afternoon, July 21, 1878, Sam Bass died. It was his 27th birthday.

$500 Reward

The above reward will be paid for the arrest and detention of **WILLIAM** (Bill) **MINER**, alias Edwards, who escaped from the New Westminster Penitentiary, at New Westminster, British Columbia, on the 8th August, 1907, where he was serving a life sentence for train robbery.

DESCRIPTION:

Age 65 years; 138 pounds; 5 feet 8½ inches; dark complexion; brown eyes; grey hair; slight build; face spotted; tattoo base of left thumb, star and ballet girl right forearm; wrist joint-bones large; moles centre of breast, 1 under left breast, 1 on right shoulder, 1 on left shoulder-blade; discoloration left buttock; scars on left shin, right leg, inside, at knee, 2 on neck.

Communicate with

LT.-COL. A. P. SHERWOOD,

Commissioner Dominion Police,
Ottawa, Canada.

BILLY MINER

10

Billy Miner

At Billy's trial one person responded this way:
"Oh Bill Miner's not so bad.
He only robs the CPR once every two years
but the CPR robs us all every day."

When the Gray Fox robbed you, you were well and truly robbed. And maybe a little bit in love. According to all accounts, the Kentucky-born Billy Miner, also known as the Gray Fox, was Canada's first train robber. A self-proclaimed pacifist, Miner was as polite and charming as they come.

"Mighty pretty dress you have on, miss. Pardon me while I take all your husband's worldly goods." Add a Southern twang, some hang-dog eyes and a handle-bar mustache, and you'll have a picture of the Most Wanted Man in New Mexico, Georgia, Colorado, Illinois, Michigan, Oregon and Washington and British Columbia.

Miner, whose dubious career spanned the end of the 19th century and the beginning of the 20th, has gained folklore status as the Gentleman Train Robber. No shoot-em'-up, pistol packin' rogue, this highwayman. But it wasn't just his impeccable manners that brought him legendary acclaim. Billy Miner was the first man to rob the Canadian Pacific

Railway, and in the eyes of the Canadian farmers, ranchers and miners who lived from the prairies to the Pacific Ocean, that was a noble thing to do.

At Billy's British Columbia trial, one person responded to a Vancouver reporter's question about public sympathy for Miner this way: "Oh, Bill Miner's not so bad. He only robs the CPR once every two years but the CPR robs us all every day."

The Canadian railway company was generally perceived in the West as a land-grabbing, money-grubbing institution that only served the interests of an elite group of Easterners. Thousands of railway-hating folks in the West protested the grain rates, the land giveaways and the intrusion of the CPR into their lives. Billy Miner tackled the big boys when he sidled up to the CPR with his gun and his grin, and his exploits induced awe and admiration in rural communities in the B.C. interior and elsewhere across the West.

Miner was born in Bowling Green, Kentucky around 1843, the son of a schoolteacher and a miner. Billy received a cursory public education before running away to become a cowboy. He arrived in San Diego at the height of the Apache War and saw it as a money-making opportunity. Unafraid to ride through hostile Native territories, Miner became a messenger for Brigadier General George Wright, delivering mail to points east of California. Because his hide was on the line, his price was high; $25 per letter accumulated quickly, and before long Billy became a big spender. To maintain the lifestyle he had quickly become accustomed to, Billy contemplated a visit to the wrong side of the law.

Young Miner decided fast money could be had ambushing slow-moving stagecoaches laden with pay packets and post or passengers flush with gold watches and silver coins. The quick-in-the-saddle Miner robbed his first coach, the Señora, in California. He must have considered the haul, $200, easy money, because Miner continued his antics until nabbed by U.S. marshals who tracked the highwayman down and captured him on April 3, 1866.

Miner was convicted on two charges of stagecoach robbery. The penalty was tough: San Quentin prison, one of the dingiest holes in the State of California, became Billy Miner's home for four years. Little did he know that he'd see the inside of San Quentin more than once in his career.

Despite its prime location just north of San Francisco, San Quentin in the mid-19th century was dismal. When Miner was released in July 1870, he had endured isolation, starvation, filthy conditions and beatings by guards and hardened criminals. He wasn't the same happy-go-lucky kid who entered San Quentin and he wasn't long for freedom. Within a year of his release he was robbing stagecoaches in Calaveros County, California, and as fate would have it, was thrown back into the black hole of San Quentin in 1871. This time, however, Miner was given a 12-year sentence for a robbery in San Andreas.

He served two years before scaling the walls in his first daring prison break. Despite being captured and thrown into solitary confinement within hours, the taste of stolen freedom must have whetted his appetite for escape, for the Gray Fox was to escape prison five times in a lifetime revolving around notorious robberies and horrific punishments.

After serving nine long years, Miner was finally released from San Quentin on July 14, 1880. In need of quick cash, the Gray Fox quickly resumed his old profession, hitching up with bandit-adventurer Billy Leroy—also known as Arthur Pond—to work the Colorado country. Miner also changed his identity. Working under the alias of William A. Morgan, he and Pond relieved the Del Norte stage of a cool $3600 in gold coin and dust. Before the stagecoach moved on, Miner, his saddlebags crammed with stolen goods, wished the driver a safe journey, knowing the treacherous country the Del Norte had to travel to reach its Salt Lake City destination. The stagecoach may be have been empty of its gold, but ever-gentlemanly Miner didn't want to see lives lost owing to careless driving.

Miner must have aspired to a gentleman's lifestyle because he adopted it easily. A change of name, a new city and a packet of stolen cash were the only things needed to establish himself with the best of upper-crust society. Although Leroy was captured and hanged from a cottonwood tree as a warning to other bandits, Miner escaped custody and by late summer of 1880 was comfortably ensconced in Onondaga, Michigan, hosting parties, courting women and living a life of genteel respectability, financed of course by his dubious "inheritances." He was known now as William Anderson, a kindly gentleman who knew how to treat a gal properly and who cut a fine figure on the dance floor.

It couldn't last. Miner excused himself from Michigan society and headed back to Colorado to exercise his chosen career, but not, according to some reports, before the entire citizenry of Onondaga came out to his farewell bash. He was charming and could draw an impressive crowd. Even as a robber, Miner was unfailingly apologetic about having to upset the stagecoach passengers. His signature manners eventually became his undoing. Authorities in the West got wind of the Gentleman Bandit and his accomplices, and a Colorado posse was formed in August 1881 to track and capture the Gray Fox and his rag-tag team of ne'er-do-wells.

Success was on the side of the law, but not completely. Miner managed to hold up stagecoaches in Arizona and California before being caught by U.S. marshals and shipped back to his old stomping grounds. He was admitted to San Quentin for a third time in December 1881. This time, after a failed attempt to escape, Miner served 20 of his 25 years in the pen. By the time he was released in 1901, Miner's livelihood was in jeopardy. Technological advances had ushered in the new century and stagecoaches had almost everywhere been replaced by trains. Labelled a troublemaker by authorities, Miner would have to watch his next move.

But it wasn't such a difficult transition for the shaggy, gray-haired criminal with the immaculate mustache. After all, a train was no more than a strung-together stagecoach with more gold and fewer people to deal with. In the mountainous terrain the slow-moving locomotives laboring up hills were little challenge to a gang of men on fresh mounts waiting in the underbrush.

Traveling north from California, Miner attempted his first train robbery near Portland, Oregon, in September 1903 at a siding called Trout Lake. Miner and his men botched their first hold up of a Great Northern Railroad train badly. It takes at least three men to rob a train—one to threaten the locomotive crew, one to intimidate the passengers and one to seize the express car where valuables are held. Because of his non-violent tendencies, Miner's task was usually the last. In this Great Northern robbery, one bandit was killed, another wounded, and in typical fashion, Miner escaped without a scratch.

He drifted north to Washington State and eventually found his way across the border to Canada in 1904. What followed was a relatively tranquil period in the life of the Gray Fox. Settling in the Nicola Valley near Kamloops, Miner re-created himself as a retired rancher who dabbled in land, owned a few cows and toyed with the notion of prospecting. He adopted the alias George Edwards and soon became known as a pleasant grandfatherly type. He was pleasant to children, kind to orphans and even gave generous donations to the church.

When George Edwards left his ranch for business in the first week of September 1904, none of his neighbors knew Billy Miner was back in the saddle. Throwing his lot in with a couple of dubious characters named Shortie Dunn, a Montana outlaw on the run from American lawmen, and Lewis (Scottie) Colquon (also spelled Colquhoan in some accounts), a small-time Ontario crook, the Billy Miner gang was formed anew. The Gray Fox's first Canadian Pacific conquest was planned and executed on Canada's West Coast.

On September 13, 1904, a CPR train, the westbound Transcontinental No. 1, loaded with gold dust from the Cariboo Gold Mine in Ashcroft, B.C., was heading down the Fraser Canyon for the coast when Miner and the gang boarded the blind baggage car just west of Mission. They crawled over the baggage, mail and express cars and shimmied into the engine room where the chief engineer, Nat Scott, felt a gun in his ribs. Miner ordered him to cut the train behind the express car, pull ahead, then cut the engine off.

From the express car safe, the Gray Fox and his accomplices netted not only the Ashcroft gold dust shipment valued at $4000, but $2000 of gold dust destined for the vault of the

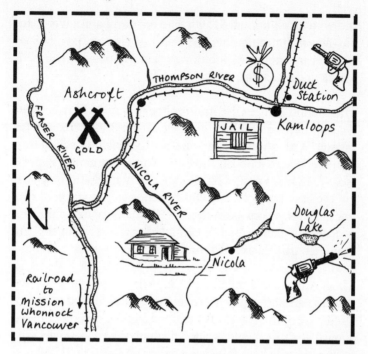

INTERIOR BRITISH COLUMBIA, CANADA

Bank of British North America in Victoria, and $914.37 in hard cash.

Delighted by their booty, the gang scooped up the profits and rode the engine three miles down the track to Whonnock, B.C. A daring leap off the train and a tumble down the steep, rocky banks to the Fraser River saw the Billy Miner gang escape.

The CPR immediately offered a reward of $5000, or $1500 per outlaw, to anybody who could provide information used to apprehend the bandits. The Canadian government sweetened the pot with more money—$6000—while the province

threw in an additional $1500. The rail companies were seri-
ous about apprehending the band of thieves, particularly
when they knew the public was secretly pleased the CPR
was taking a beating.

The second Miner CPR train robbery was on May 8, 1906.
It turned into a botched business for the Gray Fox and his
friends. With Shortie Dunn and Scotty Colquon still in tow,
Miner chose to ambush the CPR Transcontinental Express
No. 97, 15 miles east of Kamloops at Duck's Station, bypass-
ing the easy prey of a $35,000 currency shipment on nearby
tracks. He was convinced the No. 97 was carrying a shipment
of $100,000 subscribed in Canada for the relief of the San
Francisco earthquake victims. It was a costly error.

Miner ordered the train be uncoupled, and the mail car, two
express cars and engine were separated and moved to an isolated part of the tracks. When Dunn and Colquon climbed
aboard, the three bandits rifled through the express cars only
to find old mail bags. The gang ended up splitting $15.50 net-
ted from the sacks of mail bound for Victoria. Reports from
the CPR say the bandits overlooked a bag containing
$40,000 cash—the safe in the second express car also had
bullion worth the same.

Miner was a day late and a dollar short on all counts; not
only did he miss the gold and the cash, but the San Francisco
shipment had moved the previous day.

Despite the general ill-will toward the CPR, people in the
area were shocked that common bandits could interfere
with the stability and almost sacred nature of the govern-
ment-subsidized rail transportation system. With the cash
reward of almost $15,000, a huge manhunt was mounted to

bring the Gentleman Bandit and his gang to justice. They were wanted dead or alive.

The 1906 search for Billy Miner included not only common men hungry for the reward, but also hastily commissioned special constables, cowboys, American detectives, railway police, provincial officers and the Royal North-West Mounted Police. Billy Miner had no hope of going back to the Nicola Valley as George Edwards. His face was plastered on every post, beam and tree between Vancouver, Calgary and Spokane. The Gray Fox was cornered.

The Gentleman Bandit and his gang were discovered near Douglas Lake in the Nicola Valley by Provincial Constable William Fernie. Even though the trio had a fairly credible story about prospecting, something in the leader's demeanor made Fernie suspicious. He reported his conversation with the "older gentleman" to the Royal North-West Mounted Police, who decided to check out the situation for themselves.

Wasting little time, a party of Mounted Police made their way to Miner's camp. Miner, Dunn and Colquon were squirreling down a campfire meal, confident they had outwitted the law once again, when they were confronted by the authorities. When questioned about the recent CPR hold up, Miner and his gang denied having any part in it. The Mounties weren't convinced. The bluff ended when sudden cheek-to-cheek contact with the Mounties proved too much pressure for Dunn, who pulled his pistol on the posse and made a break for the bush. A round of gunfire caught him in the leg, and Miner and Colquon, realizing the game was up, surrendered themselves without protest. The three desperadoes were taken to nearby Kamloops to stand trial on charges of armed train robbery.

Miner, still claiming to be gentleman rancher George Edwards, carried his new persona through two trials; the first resulting in a hung jury and the second resulting in a quick guilty verdict. Life sentences were doled out to Dunn and Miner, and Colquon received a 25-year sentence. Despite a positive identification from the former San Quentin warden and all the evidence pointing to his past, the 64-year-old gray-haired prospector with the handlebar mustache refused to admit he was infamous stagecoach and train robber Billy Miner. Maybe it was modesty or the notion that bragging was bad manners. Whichever, Miner was sent to the New Westminster Provincial Jail protesting his innocence.

After 34 years in San Quentin prison, enduring the New Westminster prison system must have seemed like child's play to the Gray Fox. But a prison is still a prison and Miner continued to scheme his escape. In typical style, he befriended and won the trust of the deputy warden's daughter, who hoped to win his soul for Jesus through evangelical teaching and prayer. Alas, Miner had more worldly aspirations on his mind. After requesting and having been granted permission to work in the prison brickyard, Miner found what was probably the only place in the jail yard where he could not be observed from guard towers. On August 8, 1907, with the cunning of a fox and the help of three young convicts, the Gentleman Bandit dug his way under the fence and vanished beyond the walls of the prison. The Gray Fox was on the loose again.

Rumor has long circulated that Miner had help springing himself from the New Westminster Penitentiary a little over a year after receiving his life sentence. Whether he bribed prison officials or simply charmed his way to freedom is still debated, but one thing is certain: after his escape the Gray Fox headed back into the States. Many people in British

Columbia were sorry to see him go. His folk-hero status with respect to robbing the CPR, his well-mannered heists and his uncanny ability to escape the bonds of jail had drawn admiration. The citizens of Nicola Valley publicly declared they would harbor their friend George Edwards in their homes whether he was the much maligned American bandit or not.

Miner must have had a homing instinct. Back in the American South, four years later, he was once again arrested for a train robbery.

The Gentleman Bandit couldn't be kept behind bars. He escaped from the Milledgeville State Prison in Georgia on October 18, 1911 but was recaptured and died on the inside on September 2, 1913, at the age of 71.

Some say he'd tip his hat and wink as often as he'd brandish a gun, but charms aside, Billy Miner, the last of the old-fashioned highwaymen, spent 36 of his 71 years in prison plotting how he'd pull off his next great train robbery—politely.

BUTCH CASSIDY

11

Butch Cassidy and the Sundance Kid

Soon the citizens were referring to a "wild bunch" of outlaws. The label stuck. The newly christened Wild Bunch was in action, and its fame soon stretched across the West as brilliantly as the twinkling night sky.

Without a doubt, Butch Cassidy and the Sundance Kid were the last great outlaws of the Wild West. Movie and song have immortalized them, and a steady stream of writers has long sought to tell the true story of this splendid pair of robbers, who even tarried in New York City before exporting the Wild West to South America in the early 20th century.

For years, Butch and Sundance led the Wild Bunch, an ever-changing gang of outlaws linked by a common dependence on impregnable hideouts. The most famous of these hideouts was named Hole-in-the-Wall: in a desolate and intricate maze of ridges and canyons in the Bighorn Mountains of Wyoming, it offered priceless refuge to an unknown number of criminals. But the Wild Bunch also whiled away the time hiding out in Brown's Park, a rugged wilderness in northwestern Colorado, and Robbers' Roost, an expanse of dry canyons in southeastern Utah. The Wild

THE WILD BUNCH AT FORT WORTH: SUNDANCE KID (FAR LEFT), WILLIAM
CARVER, BEN KILPATRICK, HARVEY LOGAN AND BUTCH CASSIDY (FAR RIGHT)

Bunch committed a series of bank and train robberies across the western states between 1896 and 1901. The daring and flamboyant holdups left relatively few of the gang members wealthy. Most of them were killed or jailed, and the two kingpins became convinced that their only means of escaping their pursuers was to flee to the relative obscurity of the pampas of Argentina.

The central figure in this gang of train and bank robbers was Robert LeRoy Parker, born on April 13, 1866 in Beaver, Utah. He was the eldest of 13 children in a Mormon family and grew up on family homesteads near Beaver and then Circleville, Utah. By the age of 13, young Bob had already left home to earn some money for the ever-growing family. Having had little formal schooling, Parker quickly became a cowboy and began to ride with a suspected cattle rustler named Mike Cassidy.

Parker's loving mother did not approve of Mike Cassidy, and she probably wondered what could possibly have permitted such an unfavorable friendship to form in her good son's life. Two anecdotes shed some light on the question. The first centers on a pair of pants. While working on the ranch of a neighbor, Bob wore out his clothes, so he asked if he could take a day off to ride into town and buy some new trousers for himself. Permission was granted, and the day fixed. When it arrived, the young cowhand set out early. Hours later he arrived in town, dusty and tired. To his dismay, he discovered that the store was closed. Frustrated at the thought of having made the trip for nothing, he took the matter into his own hands. He broke into the building, found the pants he needed and left a note for the store owner, in which he explained his actions and his intent to return and pay for what he had taken. Unfortunately, the resolution of this arrangement involved the town marshal.

The second anecdote is merely an explanation of the first, and occurred much later. In hindsight, it shows why young Bob Parker would have been attracted to the free-wheeling, risky independence of Mike Cassidy. For a time in 1888, Parker worked for the rancher Harry Adsit at Lone Cone Mountain, near Telluride, Colorado. The cowboy got on well with his employer, and when the two got to talking one day, Adsit asked Parker why such a deft and clever cowboy as himself hadn't started up his own ranch. Parker looked at him with his sharp, clear eyes, and quietly responded that he intended to make his mark in the world, and when the right opportunity came, he would seize it.

Mike Cassidy represented a chance for young Bob to get what he needed. When Mike introduced his apprentice to Cap Brown, the most famous rustler of Utah's notorious Robbers' Roost area, Bob was quick to accept the job of driving a herd of Brown's horses into Colorado. Robbers' Roost was a wild, arid landscape of hills and canyons, and it was the haunt of many a Utah badman. The job took Bob northeast from there, over the San Rafael Desert, across the Green and mighty Colorado Rivers, around the La Sal Mountains, and up the narrow valleys of the Dolores and San Miguel Rivers to the mining town of Telluride in southeastern Colorado. There, under the tall cliffs enclosing the narrow river, Bob Parker met Matt Warner and the McCarty brothers.

Rumor has it that Tom and Bill McCarty introduced Bob Parker to robbing trains. No one really knows who was in the gang that held up the Denver and Rio Grande Express in the fall of 1887, but bandits did attack that day, and money was stolen. The story that subsequently developed from these two facts shows Parker at his best.

Allegedly, he was among the outlaws of the McCarty gang, which included Matt Warner, Tom O'Day, "Silver Tip" Maxwell and "Indian Ed" Newcomb, when it saddled up and rode out into a bitterly cold and rainy wind on November 3, 1887. Despite the weather, the men picked their way north to Grand Junction on the Colorado River. They stopped the train with a few well-placed rocks on the main line. A brave express guard confronted them and barred their entry to the booty. Bill McCarty held a pistol to the guard's head and asked the assembled badmen what his fate should be. Parker diplomatically suggested a vote. In the cold and driving rain, following the ancient tradition of democracy, each gang member dutifully raised or lowered his hand according to his conviction, and the decision fell in favor of the obstinate guard. Murder was not in the gang's best interest. The bandits retreated from the robbery with the odd piece of registered mail and clear consciences.

For the next year or so, Parker worked as a cowboy at the Adsit ranch and occasionally as a miner at the gold, lead and silver mines nearby. His next dealings with the McCarty gang resulted in his change of name.

Parker hooked up with Tom McCarty again in June 1889, and they successfully held up the San Miguel Valley Bank in Telluride, Colorado. The gang, whose third member was Matt Warner, fled west toward Utah. Their pursuers were stymied by ingenious, non-violent tactics. One troop was sent scurrying by a simple note left on the trail: it warned that anyone who persisted in the chase would be shot. Another heard the sound of a company crashing through the woods at night, in apparently the opposite direction from the expected one. The alerted lawmen thought the bandits were trying to double back, and gave chase. Despite the darkness, they eventually caught up with their prey. It turned out to be a single pony with a large bunch of branches tied to its saddle. As the branches snapped, the riderless beast had plunged on, terrified, and created the sound of half a dozen desperate riders. Still more pursuers were thrown off the scent when the outlaws tied sacks to the hooves of their mounts, thus eliminating their hoofprints. Despite an extensive and prolonged manhunt by innumerable posses of lawmen, the bandits always managed to stay ahead of their would-be captors. The flight took them all the way north to Diamond Peak, on the Wyoming border, before leading back again to the relative security of Robbers' Roost in Utah. While in the Roost, Parker was tempted to visit his family again, but when he learned that the Telluride robbery had already disgraced him in the community where he had grown up, he skipped the visit and changed his name to Cassidy in deference to the rustler who had taken him under his wing. The moniker Butch would come a little while later, perhaps from a stint as a butcher. His identity had suffered an irrevocable change with the Telluride robbery. He was now an outlaw.

Butch Cassidy, Matt Warner and Tom McCarty felt so secure in the heat-baked landscape of Robbers' Roost that they even rescued a party of lawmen that was tracking them. They spied the posse at a fork in the trail. Intrigued, they watched as the evidently thirsty lawmen tried to decide which route would most quickly lead to water. When the lawmen chose wrong and headed off into an endless desert and their certain doom, Warner rushed down to where they had stood, fired his rifle for attention, and left a note explaining where water was to be had. When the lawmen reached the spring, they drank like thirsty camels.

The gesture might have been a momentary truce, but the outlaws knew that it would not hold for long. Determined to shake the law from their heels, they set a course for Wyoming.

Once in the new state, Butch Cassidy returned for a time to ranching. He acquired some land in the upper Wind River area, northwest of Lander, and made friends among the other homesteaders there. The winter of 1889 was mercilessly cold and Butch soon turned to the rustling business with another cowboy living on the fringe of the law, Al Hainer.

Meanwhile, tension mounted in Wyoming, and Butch Cassidy found himself right in the middle of it. His sentiments lay with the small homesteaders, who regularly pilfered from the big, faceless corporate ranches to stay afloat. As his reputation as a horse rustler grew, so too did the knowledge of his character. Butch's word was known to be as true as well-tempered steel. He would never rob a rancher who hired him as a cowboy, so the corporate ranches scrambled to get him on their payroll. Thus Cassidy and Hainer "sold" protection to the big ranchers, by working for them. It was the ranchers' own idea, but the ranchers must have resented it; paying suspected rustlers to protect herds of livestock never lost the flavor of extortion. When the opportunity came to nab Butch, his enemies seized it.

In August 1891, one Billy Nutcher ran into Butch in the Owl Creek Mountains. Nutcher was from Lander. He sold his old neighbor three pretty horses, without specifying their origin. If Cassidy had had his wits about him, he would have refused the sale. The horses were stolen, and they belonged to large Wyoming ranches. Before too long, the missing horses were seen among Butch's and Hainer's stock.

John Chapman and Bob Calverly were assigned to track the two down and capture them. The lawmen surprised the unarmed and unsuspecting Hainer outside a cabin and tied him securely to a tree. Then they gingerly approached the dilapidated log structure with their guns drawn. Calverly pushed open the door and sprang into the room, catching Butch Cassidy unarmed and waking from a nap.

Butch dove for his gunbelt. It lay on a table on the other side of the small room. Calverly fired four rapid shots at the lunging figure. Blue smoke filled the room. Cassidy was not killed, but a bullet grazed his scalp and knocked him unconscious. When he awoke, he found himself bound beside his companion.

The trial of the outlaws was tedious and confusing. After a year of delays, Cassidy and Hainer were acquitted of having stolen a horse from the Grey Bull Cattle Company (knowingly buying stolen goods was tantamount to stealing). But shortly before the verdict, the tactic of the prosecution became clear: another charge was brought against them. This time the plaintiff was Richard Ashworth, and the horse in question was not the same as the first. As a result of these changes, a whole new trial began. It dragged on, as the first had, and this time the result was not as favorable. In 1894, Butch Cassidy, grand outlaw and perpetrator of the Telluride robbery, was convicted for having stolen a horse worth five dollars. He was sentenced to two years in the penitentiary at Laramie, Wyoming. Hainer, once Cassidy was proved to have made the purchase, got off without punishment.

Three-quarters of the way through his sentence, Cassidy petitioned the governor, William Richards, for a pardon. Their conversation has grown into a legend that goes something like this:

"I've served most of my time," Butch said as he faced the governor in the prison administration office. "I've got some land in Colorado and it needs attention, so I'm requesting that you commute the rest of my sentence."

"If you really intend to make an honest living, something could be arranged," Williams mused. "I think you are young enough and smart enough." He paused, coughing slightly and resettling himself in the uncomfortable chair. "And I hope you have learned from your past mistakes, so if you give me your word that you will walk a straight and narrow path, I will see what I can do."

Cassidy leaned over the narrow table separating them and stared intently at the governor. "Sorry Governor, but I can't promise you that I won't ever turn back to rustling or other misdemeanors. But if you let me go, I'll give you my word that I will stay on the right side of the law in your state."

Impressed by the integrity and the startling frankness of Cassidy's response, the governor looked at him, and then waved for the guards to remove him. Within days he had signed the pardon. Cassidy walked out of jail a free man on January 19, 1896.

Once free, Cassidy rode hard for Diamond Peak, in the northeastern corner of Colorado, where his chum Matt Warner now had a respectable ranch. There he met some men who would later become integral members of the Wild Bunch. Elzy Lay was a debonair mischief-maker and a handsome ladies' man. Henry "Bub" Meeks was a young, Mormon cowboy disillusioned with the tedious routine of farm work. They soon rallied around Cassidy's natural leadership, which emerged when his friend, Matt Warner, got himself into the sort of trouble that only a highfalutin city lawyer could solve.

During Cassidy's time in jail, Warner had married a pretty girl named Rose Morgan. After their daughter Hayda was born, Warner managed to straighten out his crooked ways and assumed the responsibilities of an honest living. Ironically, his reform was rewarded with disaster: Rose went to a doctor complaining of a prolonged pain in her knee and was told that she had cancer. Before long, her leg had to be amputated. While visiting his recuperating wife in Vernal, Utah one day, Warner—understandably vulnerable on account of his wife's condition—was approached by Mr. E.B. Coleman, who offered him $100 dollars if he would help Coleman pack and move the equipment of a small mining operation high up in the Uintah Mountains. Thinking of his needy wife, Matt quickly agreed. What Coleman did not tell him was that the equipment did not belong to him.

Unfortunately, the real owners were present when Warner, accompanied by Coleman and his associate Bill Wall, arrived at the camp, and naturally they proved more than a little unwilling to hand over their property when Coleman demanded it. The real matter at stake amounted to more than a few spades and pickaxes: Coleman was almost sure of striking gold in the area soon, and he was afraid that this other group would beat him to it. Angry words quickly transformed themselves into speeding bullets, and before anyone (besides Coleman) really understood what was happening, the grim battle was decided. The miners lay stretched out upon the earth, and Matt Warner, Wall and Coleman were charged with murder. Warner stood trial in Ogden, Utah, and he needed the help of at least one good lawyer if he hoped to present the truth.

While Warner languished in prison, word came from Cassidy. Butch would make sure that Warner had the best

Utah lawyers that money could buy. Where that money would come from, the note did not explain.

Cassidy's almost two years in jail had given him firsthand knowledge of the consequences of being unprepared. He had also heard that his former associate, Bill McCarty, had been shot to pieces in an ill-planned raid on a bank in Delta, Colorado, in September 1893. Cassidy never wanted to have to return to the squalor and confinement of jail; in all his jobs he stressed the importance of planning, diligence and organization to the men around him. A little cunning would get him the money to free his friend.

On August 13, 1896, Butch Cassidy, Elzy Lay and Bub Meeks rode into the peaceful town of Montpelier, Idaho. Butch and his pals had prepared themselves by working (under false names) on a nearby ranch, but after two weeks of harvesting, their familiarity with the town and its surrounding landscape was complete. One of them stayed outside with the horses. The other two walked up the boardwalk, pulled their bandannas over their faces and strode into the bank.

"Put your hands up, and face the wall!" ordered Butch. As the terrified citizens complied, Elzy danced around the counter to the cashier.

"Gimme all your bills," ordered Elzy. He glanced down. At the man's feet was a Winchester rifle.

The cashier swallowed. "There are none here, sir," he gulped.

"God-damn liar!" swore Elzy, and struck the man on the forehead with his pistol.

"Don't you dare hit him again!" shouted Butch from his position at the door. The surprised customers, on whom his pistol was trained, looked around curiously. "Face the wall," Butch repeated angrily. They complied. Elzy, meanwhile, had gotten his hands on a wad of money, and was stuffing it into his bag. He swiped a pile of gold coins sitting on a nearby table, and, for good measure, plucked the Winchester from its place on the ground. He then ambled toward the door.

"If you all stay put for 10 good minutes, no one will get hurt," warned Butch, as he and Elzy backed out of the building. They then leapt to their horses—a witness to the Telluride robbery had earlier testified that she had seen young Bob Parker practice the trick for weeks before that heist, to the confusion of his horse and the endless amusement of secret onlookers—and rode out of town. They had struck like lightning, and scooped up over $7000 dollars.

Lawyers D.N. Straupp and Orlando W. Powers were hired to defend Matt Warner. They succeeded in dispelling the charges of murder, but Warner was still sentenced to five years in jail for manslaughter. E.B. Coleman walked away free. Butch's observation that justice is best served in the saddle and not the courts seemed once more to carry weight.

Butch, Elzy and Bub retreated to the relatively wild land around Diamond Peak, where they spent Thanksgiving with the Bassett family. The Bassetts had taken Butch in during the flight after the Telluride robbery, and their daughter Ann was sweet on him. To show their gratitude, the outlaws announced their intent to serve the dinner to their hosts. Ann laughed delightedly as the embarrassed Butch clumsily slopped coffee on the clean, white tablecloth.

"My, my," she remarked dryly, "To think that simple eti-quette could strike so much fear into the heart of such a brave man as yourself!"

Butch fled to the kitchen, where he was consoled by his comrades.

Despite their happiness with the Bassetts, the outlaws opted to ride south to the safety of Robbers' Roost. They made their camp in the badlands of Horseshoe Canyon. Butch planned another robbery for the spring of 1897. It took place in Castle Gate, in northwestern Carbon County, Utah, over 100 miles northwest of their lair. With the help of Elzy Lay and Joe Walker, he intercepted the payroll of an entire mining camp. Without firing a single shot, the bandits made off with a smooth sense of victory and $8000. They skirted the towns of Helper and Price to avoid the posses and soon reached the security of the Roost, where no lawman dared follow them.

Everyone knew who had committed the robbery at Castle Gate. But no one could catch him. Butch Cassidy was becom-ing a man with a reputation. Floating on the currency taken at Castle Gate, and looking for a less isolated place to spend it, Butch drifted back up toward Diamond Peak. The constel-lation of men around him now grew to eight or nine. Besides Elzy Lay and Bub Meeks, the gang included Harvey "Kid Curry" Logan, "Flat Nose" George Currie and Harry Alonzo Longabaugh. Castle Gate marked the beginning; the relation-ships began to solidify thereafter. Soon the citizens of Vernal, Utah were fearfully referring to a "wild bunch" of outlaws inhabiting Brown's Park, which was what they called the land around Diamond Peak. The label stuck. The newly christened Wild Bunch was in action, and its fame soon stretched across the West as brilliantly as the twinkling night sky.

Longabaugh had gravitated to Brown's Park circuitously, drifting west from his birthplace in Pennsylvania through a number of crimes before discovering the secure hideout. In 1887, he had been arrested by Sheriff James Ryan in Miles City, Montana for the theft of a number of horses from the VVV ranch in Crook County, northeastern Wyoming, where he had been working. Brought back to the county seat of Sundance, Longabaugh served 18 months in jail. It was enough to brand him with a tenacious nickname. Harry "The Sundance Kid" Longabaugh hooked up with the Wild Bunch shortly thereafter. Changed perhaps by prison, he was a taciturn and moody man, and a stark contrast to the outgoing, personable Cassidy. Nevertheless, the two got along well and eventually became inseparable. Butch Cassidy and the Sundance Kid would be together at the end.

The next bank robbery by the Wild Bunch took place in Belle Fourche, South Dakota, on June 28, 1897. One of the gang members, Tom O'Day, was captured at the scene of this crime. A posse relentlessly set out after the other gang members, but they split up once they reached Wyoming and eluded capture. The nucleus of the Wild Bunch remained intact. The outlaws crashed into Dixon later that summer to celebrate. The Saturday-night revelers on the main street ran for cover when the gang members began to discharge their guns. Swollen with power and whiskey, they pranced around on horseback, firing their bullets at the stars.

In 1898, war broke out between the United States and Spain over the fate of Cuba. The American battleship *Maine* was sunk in the harbor of Havana, and the resultant drowning of over 250 American naval officers sparked a fiery, patriotic response. During the conflict, the Wild Bunch refrained from criminal activity. Butch even sent a letter to the Governor of Wyoming, William Richards, who had granted him the pardon three years before. In the letter, he promised that none of his men would cause any trouble while the country was at war. Some members of the Bunch may have even signed up as soldiers.

By the next year, the Spanish-American War was over and the Wild Bunch got back to work. The members decided to start with the Overland Flyer of the Union Pacific Railroad. Cassidy had experience from his days with the McCarty boys, but for many of the others the heist would be their first foray into robbing trains.

In the dead of night on June 2, 1899, four men boarded the train that was coming from Omaha at the little station of Wilcox, which lay about a dozen miles southeast of Medicine Bow, Wyoming. As the streaming night air slipped over their bodies, they slithered forward on top of the cars until they reached the locomotive. They plunged down upon the engineer and commanded him to stop the train as soon as it had crossed the trestle bridge coming up. Bravely, the engineer turned his eyes back to the track. The train sped forward into the cold darkness. Soon the far side of the canyon flickered into view, faintly illuminated by the headlight. As the train left the bridge, the engineer braked. Up ahead was a bobbing red lantern.

Taking the engineer and the fireman hostage, the four robbers jumped to the ground, where they were joined by two more. The party walked back to the mail car and demanded that it be opened. The two clerks, Burt Bruce and Robert Lawson, at first refused, but when the floor shuddered from the force of an explosion they quickly changed their minds.

Little money was found among the letters, but before the out-laws could proceed to the express car, a light appeared on the track behind them. Another train was coming from Wilcox.

The men with the guns acted fast. The leader barked out orders, and the others jumped to perform them. One dealt out sticks of dynamite to a partner. These two then raced back onto the bridge. The others climbed aboard the engine, and moved the train a short way forward. An artificial thunderclap left little doubt in the mind of the trembling engineer about what had just happened. After the two pyrotechnists had returned, the engine and express car were separated from the rest of the train and moved another two miles down the track to be assaulted without interruption.

The gang walked up to the express car and ordered the guard inside to open the door. His response was mystifying:

"Come and get me!"

The express car guard, E.C. Woodcock, must not have known that the gang possessed more dynamite or he might have been more accommodating. The fuse was lit. Its light showed Sundance looking to Butch for confirmation. Cassidy nodded.

Harry tossed the dynamite onto the tracks. The fuse hissed, and the gang ducked for cover. A fierce blast rocked the express car and tore it open, sending papers, metal and banknotes flying every which way. Woodcock was hurled to the ground, but he was not killed by the force of the explosion. Harvey Logan loomed out of the shadow, pulled his gun and advanced. Woodcock lay stunned and bleeding on the ground. "This damned fellow is going to hell!" he shouted, cocking the firearm. The night held its breath as if in anticipation of the summary execution. Cassidy, however, intervened.

"Harvey, the man is courageous and injured. With nerves like that he doesn't deserve to be shot."

The Wild Bunch gathered the scattered banknotes and stuffed the cash into saddlebags and gunnysacks. Then they faded away from the disabled train into the enveloping gloom. The take from the spectacular robbery was at least $30,000 and perhaps as much as $60,000.

After the outlaws had vanished, it began to rain. Dawn came slowly to Wyoming that day. The train limped into Medicine Bow, and the engineer telegraphed for help.

Within a day, Sheriff Joe Hazen was in Casper, Wyoming heading up a force of ready lawmen. The posse was not given much chance to confer, for on June 4 word came that the outlaws had been spotted at a cabin on Casper Creek, a mere six miles away. Led by Hazen, 11 indignant law-enforcers swung astride their mounts and galloped out of town.

The cabin was of course deserted by the time they reached it, but a clear track had been left by the fleeing outlaws, who numbered no more than three. Before long, Sheriff Hazen had engaged them in a gun battle. The outlaws decided to make a stand.

"Give yourselves up!" shouted Hazen. "You're cornered and outnumbered!" The outlaws responded by shooting at the posse. Alternating their attacks, the lawmen closed in until they could hear the outlaws cursing and muttering.

Hazen looked down at his gun. He could smell the metal in his sweaty hand. The handle seemed to be pulsing in syncopation with his heart, and the taste in his mouth was somehow metallic. The device was heavy: the frame, the hammer, the cylinder, the barrel and the trigger all added up to a deadliness that he could hardly fathom, but which now pressed itself, wordless, upon his senses.

A close blast jolted him from his contemplation. "Coward," he muttered at himself, and mustered his courage. Then he charged.

A bullet from one of the Wild Bunch caught him in the stomach. He doubled over, flipped back and fell to the ground. His men rallied around him and rushed him back to Casper, but he had lost too much blood by the time he arrived. He died before the sun set twice on his wound. The three outlaws escaped.

Baffled and dismayed by the masterful crime, the Union Pacific Railroad Company brought in scores of Pinkerton detectives and hired the best bounty hunters to track down and capture the audacious bandits. The death of the well-known and affable Hazen enraged the citizens of Wyoming. Dozens of posses led by lawmen like the famous Charles Siringo and W.O. Sayles scoured the desolate reaches of the state. They followed various leads south, and were sure they were on the right track, until a discovery in Montana drew them north again. Detectives meticulously gathered information and transcribed the eyewitness accounts of the passengers. Newspapermen were let in on the details and in melodramatic language alerted the nation to the identities and activities of the thieves. The forces of the law never wanted to be embarrassed by the criminals of the Wilcox robbery again.

Butch Cassidy, meanwhile, was quietly working as a cowboy named Jim Lowe on a ranch near Alma, New Mexico, in the winding valley of the San Francisco River.

Elzy Lay also worked on the ranch near Alma, and he too had an alias. But he did not have Butch's patience and could not stay put. When the chance came, Elzy Lay decided to hook up with the notorious "Black Jack" Ketchum and his gang to rob yet another train. They held up the Colorado Southern Railroad near Folsom, New Mexico. This heist was not as well planned, and Lay and Ketchum were quickly tracked down. In the fierce gunfight that followed, Sheriff Edward Farr was shot dead by the outlaws. Both Lay and Ketchum were wounded. The former was cornered by lawmen and captured after another running gunfight. He was sentenced to life and served his time at the New Mexico Territorial Prison. Eventually paroled, Elzy Lay passed away in 1936. His confederate, Ketchum, was hunted down as well. His death was not nearly as gentle; he was captured and gruesomely hanged in a botched execution.

The conviction of Elzy Lay shook Butch's confidence. Elzy had shared happy times with Butch and the two had got along like a house on fire in the Montpelier and Castle Gate robberies. Now the flashy Elzy, whose debonair response to challenges both criminal and romantic had always been a dark smirk, was behind bars for life.

Bub Meeks, the other man at Montpelier, had also been captured and was serving a 35-year sentence. At this point, Butch Cassidy considered turning himself in and going straight. He even went as far as setting in motion some procedures that might have led to his reform and a general pardon. But before they could be culminated, they were derailed by chance.

On a midsummer day in 1900, Butch Cassidy climbed up to the road in Lost Soldier Pass. If the planned conversation was a trap, or if it somehow went awry, he figured that he had a reasonable chance at a getaway. Douglas Preston, his lawyer and friend from the time of the trial over the five-dollar horse, had arranged for him to meet with some of the top dogs of the Union Pacific Railroad. His ingenious plan was to get Butch a pardon from the company, in hopes that the governors of Wyoming, Idaho and Colorado would be impressed by the subsequent wave of peace, and follow suit. The truce would be a simple matter of shaking hands; Butch's word was known to be true.

The sun rose in the sky, and began to sink. Any minute now, the buckboard would come toiling up the road, drawing a long tail of dust. Butch climbed up to a rise above the road and looked south, waiting for that buckboard with Preston and the others. His fugitive's eyes scouted out the features of the land. As he waited through the long, hot day he wondered what lay beyond New Mexico? Old Mexico. Panama. South America. These were names without meaning to him.

Finally, Cassidy walked down from the rock. The time of the meeting had come and gone. The sun was sinking, and a whipping wind was running before an approaching storm. Butch pulled a paper out of his pocket, and calmly wrote the following words:

"Damn you Preston, you have double-crossed me. I waited all day but you didn't show up. Tell the U.P. to go to hell. And you can go with them."

And then he left Lost Soldier Pass. South America was in his eyes.

In August, Butch and the Sundance Kid planned another train robbery. They had learned that the No. 3 Union Pacific would be carrying a considerable amount of cash when it passed through Tipton in south-central Wyoming. With Harvey Logan and possibly two other members of the Wild Bunch, Cassidy and Sundance set out from the ranch of a friend near Dixon and halted the train on August 29, 1900.

In an ironic twist of fate, the express car guard was the very same man who had resisted them near Wilcox. Woodcock again refused to open the door. An exasperated Butch threatened to blow up the whole train. It was only the pleading of the engineer that persuaded the plucky guard to open the express car door. The Wild Bunch blew open the safe with dynamite and made off with $55,000. It was their biggest haul to date.

In September of that same year, Cassidy led the Wild Bunch across the steppes and deserts of northern Utah and Nevada to Winnemuca, where, on the 19th, a mere 20 days after the Tipton robbery, they robbed the bank of $30,000.

The law was steadily closing in. Detective Charles Siringo had picked up the scent again after the Tipton robbery, and this time he was making startling discoveries. He almost caught Butch Cassidy and the Sundance Kid in Fort Worth, Texas, when carelessness or frivolity led the outlaws to have their photo taken there by a man named John Swartz. Swartz was so proud of the portrait of the snappy strangers that he hung a copy in his front window. A passer-by realized who the men were and alerted the authorities. The picture of "the Fort Worth Five"—showing, from left to right, Harry Longabaugh, Will Carver, Ben Kilpatrick, Harvey Logan and Butch Cassidy—was quickly recognized as a priceless clue in the hunt for the Wild Bunch, and agents of the law swarmed into town. Luckily for them, the outlaws had already left for San Antonio.

In San Antonio, the Sundance Kid fell in love with a woman named Etta Place. Of all the stories linked to the Wild Bunch, hers is the most obscure. She may have been a disaffected wife and teacher looking for adventure. Many accounts link her to a fancy brothel named Fanny's, which Butch and Sundance were known to frequent when they were in San Antonio. Some even say that Etta hailed from the East, and that she knew Harry Longabaugh long before he became the Sundance Kid. At any rate, their mutual affection virtually married them, and Butch recognized that all future plans would include her.

Seeing that the lawmen would eventually find them, and weary of the pattern of heated pursuit and nervous waiting, Butch Cassidy planned one final train robbery. It would provide him and Longabaugh with the money they needed to leave the increasingly populated American West. They hoped to forget the Pinkerton detectives and settle down to a placid, respectable ranching life in South America.

Butch Cassidy was all too aware of the escalating danger in the outlaws' life. Posses did not always catch bandits immediately, but they did not forget about them either, and each subsequent crime added only that much more certainty to the evidence gathered from the last. Law was a patient animal, which sooner or later caught its prey. Under these cumulative circumstances, capture was only a matter of time. Furthermore, the railroads were increasingly pulling extra boxcars filled with teams of heavily armed rangers if the train was to run anywhere near the outlaws' territory. Wanted posters were plastered in every small town across the West—the Fort Worth photo was proving very costly.

THE SUNDANCE KID AND ETTA PLACE

Moreover, the small towns were multiplying. Once-uninhabited stretches were now speckled with lights at night, and the already established settlements were beginning to feel crowded to men who had grown up with only a few neighbors. Cassidy sensed the end of an era was close at hand. He intended to make one final statement and then leave the continent forever.

Before doing so, however, he did something thoroughly unexpected. The act is such a surprise, even to modern historians on the outlaw trail, that no one can really decide on the exact dates or course of events. Butch Cassidy, the Sundance Kid and the beautiful Etta Place, whom Sundance intended to take to South America, shook the dust of the West from their shoes, and took a break. They went to New York City. There they stayed for more than three weeks, adding one of the most surprising chapters to the history of the Wild West. They luxuriated in the city's finer hotels, took in the sights of Times Square and Manhattan, and relaxed. Basking in an extravagance unknown to them before then, they strolled the wide boulevards and blended with the crowds, ate at fine restaurants, and went shopping.

Butch made plans to meet Harry and Etta in South America some time during the following year. The couple sailed on the British freighter SS *Herminius* in February 1901, and arrived in Buenos Aires some time in March; Butch, meanwhile, headed west again.

The Wild Bunch assembled one last time. Rather than risk another attack on the Union Pacific, they chose the Great Northern Railroad, which was not yet offering dead-or-alive rewards for captured bandits. They would hit it just before the lonely town of Wagner, Montana. Harvey Logan rode with Butch that day, as did Ben "The Tall Texan" Kilpatrick and a man named Camilla Hanks.

The outlaws took up their positions east of Wagner on the cloudless, scorching hot day of July 3, 1901. It was the eve of the national holiday, but the targeted Great Northern Flyer was carrying more than just fireworks. Kilpatrick and Harvey Logan boarded the train as it picked up speed leaving the station of Malta. Logan then hooked on to the second car, clambered over the coal tender and, with a pistol in each hand, dropped down on the startled engineer, whom he commanded to stop the train.

The train ground to a shuddering halt at the switch outside of Wagner, where Cassidy and Hanks were waiting. Sticking to his usual *modus operandi*, Butch laid a stick of dynamite underneath the express safe and blew off its side. The bandits grabbed over $40,000, most of which consisted of unsigned banknotes. Then, after firing parting shots into the air, the Wild Bunch sprinted for the safety of their horses and departed. They outstripped the lumbering posses that were formed to pursue them, split the money at the first opportunity, and then went their separate ways.

Ben Kilpatrick and his girlfriend Laura Bullion headed east. They were arrested in Knoxville, Tennessee with some of the banknotes from the Wagner robbery. Both received lengthy jail terms. Upon his release, Kilpatrick found the lure of robbery too strong to resist. He was shot dead by an express guard in the course of a failed train robbery in 1912. Harvey Logan was also imprisoned in Knoxville for a time, but then escaped. Lawmen hunted him down and cornered him. Trapped and wounded, Logan fired a bullet into his brain rather than be taken alive.

The Wild Bunch, the most organized and efficient group of criminals ever to have operated in the West, had disintegrated like grass in a prairie fire.

Butch escaped. Some time later in 1901, or in early 1902, he sailed to South America. He was probably welcomed by Harry and Etta when he arrived in Buenos Aires; an official request to buy some government land in the remote Chubut province was made in Buenos Aires in April 1902, and bore the signatures of Butch and Sundance. (The aliases they used, James Ryan and Harry A. Place, were later exposed by Pinkerton agents.) The three then traveled south together by train to Patagonia. Seemingly infinite, and infinitely remote, it was everything Butch had wanted. Farms were sparse, and neighbors could be a day's ride away. The language of the other passengers on the train was somehow exhilarating too: to Butch, who understood little of it, it added to the exotic cloak of secrecy which the fugitives had finally won for themselves. The three émigrés obtained 25,000 acres in the province of Chubut, and during the first winter, they homesteaded on their new land. Cassidy spent much of the first winter alone because Etta preferred the more civilized attractions of the city to a canvas tent strung over rough-hewn logs. Butch was a stranger in a strange land, but the isolation could hardly have been oppressive, seasoned as it was with the relief of not being hunted by the Pinkerton detectives. He was living the life that he had once envisioned years ago in the darkness of a Wyoming prison. Butch started building a home that would be comfortable and cozy for "the family of three."

A relatively carefree year passed. The outlaws ranched and farmed, marveling in the vastness of the Cholila Valley. Sadly, the idyllic existence would not last. Cassidy proved that one could take a man out of the Wild West, but not the Wild West out of the man.

SOUTH AMERICA

In 1903, the Pinkerton National Detective Agency sent agent Frank Dimaio to Buenos Aires after having heard that the notorious outlaws were living in Argentina. Dimaio made some discreet inquiries and ascertained that the gringos living in Patagonia were none other than Butch Cassidy and the Sundance Kid. Delayed by the rainy season, the Pinkerton agent made sure that local authorities were well supplied with translated wanted posters of the three, and notified headquarters that the outlaws were residing in the Cholila Valley. Pinkerton authorities applauded Dimaio for his work, but told him that they were having trouble drumming up support for an effective capture; the big railroads seemed pleased that Butch and Sundance were in another hemisphere and had no desire to see them brought back.

The ranch in Cholila grew to a respectable size. By 1905, it boasted a small staff, out-buildings, a store, and huge herds of cattle and sheep. Something was not quite right, though. The beautiful days passed too quickly, too predictably. Not being able to speak Spanish well had proved more disadvantageous than they thought. Did the gradual dissipation of their hard-earned funds cause Butch Cassidy and the Sundance Kid to rethink their position? Or was a deeper need at the root of their next action? Haunted by shadows of past holdups, and the danger, the anxiety, the adrenaline-pumping thrill of success that they had entailed, Butch Cassidy and the Sundance Kid decided to give up the quiet life and leap back into action.

On Valentine's Day, 1905, two men strode into the sleepy, quiet bank in Río Gallegos, near the Straits of Magellan at the southern tip of Argentina, and demanded all the money in the safe, threatening that the uncooperative would pay with their lives. The orders were given in an awkward Spanish.

"Put your hands up and keep them raised high!" barked the taller of the two, as his masked companion rifled through drawers and the opened safe. The clock on the wall showed 11 o'clock in the morning. Flies buzzed through the hot air. The bank clerks and the manager stood rigid as the pistol-waving banditos rummaged through the contents of the vault. Within four minutes the two men were backing out the gilt-edged frosted doors, and a scuffling in the dust followed by the pound of hooves marked their escape. The men were never identified. But those who heard of the holdup and had seen the wanted posters had no doubt that it signaled the return of Butch Cassidy and the Sundance Kid.

Whether or not they were the perpetrators of the robbery, Butch and Sundance were suspects. Tipped off by a sympathetic sheriff enamored with Etta, the trio avoided being captured by Argentinean police by heading north and sailing across Lake Nahuel Huapi to Chile aboard the steamer *Condor.* They cooled their heels in Antofagasta, a mining center on the nitrate reserves at the edge of the northern desert. Then they returned briefly to Argentina.

Etta disguised herself as a man and got a taste of the action of outlawry, when, with a fourth, unidentified person, Butch Cassidy and the Sundance Kid held up the bank at Villa Mercedes, 400 miles west of Buenos Aires. It was their last robbery in Argentina, and it rewarded them with 12,000 pesos. They retreated hastily in the middle of a blinding storm across the snow-covered Andes back to the relative safety of Chile.

A few months later, the Sundance Kid said his final goodbyes to Etta Place, who was sailing for the United States. Some accounts suggest that she needed an appendix operation; others say that she had become pregnant and could no longer endure the hectic existence of the fugitive. Whatever the reason, she departed and faded out of the sphere of outlaw history, which, like the cloak of a comet, continued to illuminate Butch Cassidy and the Sundance Kid.

Cassidy meandered north to Bolivia and eventually found work at the Concordia Tin Mines, which were nestled in the Bolivian Andes, 16,000 feet above sea level. He worked as an outrider, miner and guard under the name of Santiago Maxwell. Sundance found work driving mules from northern Argentina to La Paz, Bolivia, but he grew tired of the monotonous job and joined Cassidy at Concordia. The two outlaws gradually established a guarded friendship with the boss of the mine, Rolla Glass, and an American mining engineer named Percy Seibert.

"They were two fine fellows," Seibert reminisced. "Butch was the more open and friendly of the two, the Kid being pretty quiet and at times aloof. I knew they were outlaws, but I never had the slightest bit of trouble with either of them. Glass even trusted them with the delivery of the payroll, and they always delivered every last cent of it."

Soon Glass retired, and Seibert took his place. Upon his promotion to the position of manager, he invited Butch and Sundance to join him for Sunday dinner at his hacienda. Thereafter, the outlaws often visited him. Cassidy loved the music that Seibert played on his gramophone. It appeared to relax him. But he always took the chair that afforded the best view of the valley and the trail leading up to the house.

Their stay at the Concordia mine did not last. Driven ever onward by their inner fire, Butch and the Sundance Kid headed east into the tropical savanna that formed the heartland of Bolivia. From Santa Cruz, Cassidy sent a letter to the English-speaking immigrants he had befriended during the settled time in Argentina. In burning language, it raved about the beauty of the frontier towns.

Butch Cassidy was now 41 years old.

The pair had left the Concordia Mining Company in 1908, and their drifting ultimately brought them to the Aramayo, Francke y Compañia mining camp near Tupiza, a town in southern Bolivia. They were restless.

"We've got to make a move soon, Harry," observed Butch. "We can't go back to Seibert's. Too many people have suspicions there. Argentina's out too. Basically we're lookin' at a quick hit here, and then a dash across the border to Chile or Peru. Heck, fame and fortune should be a blessing, not a curse." They settled on robbing the Aramayo office of its payroll.

The two rose before dawn the next day and trekked up Dead Cow Hill (known as Huaca Huañusca to the locals). They ensconced themselves in a bend in the tortuous path, from which they impatiently marked the laborious progress of the mules with the payroll toward them. Finally, the moment arrived. Stepping onto the path in front of their target, the remaining two members of the Wild Bunch leveled their weapons at the surprised escort and politely asked for the mine payroll. They spoke in English, but their intent was clear.

Carlos Peró, entrusted with delivering the miners' money, blinked at the sight of the two heavily armed foreigners. "The regular payroll is coming tomorrow," he stammered. "All that is in the saddlebags is 15,000 pesos."

Cassidy was taken aback. Had he miscalculated? He had expected almost five times that amount. Quickly recovering, he removed the cash and, for good measure, took one of the burros. The Sundance Kid retreated into the background, wordless. Butch Cassidy waved his rifle as a signal that the men might leave. The bandits then sidled off up the hill.

At the nearest town, Peró reported the robbery to bystanders and the local police. By means of both message-runners and a rudimentary telegraph system, the word spread and within hours soldiers, police and armed bands of miners were scouring the countryside for the Americans. No mountain road, no valley, no train station was without a patrol.

Butch and the Kid were being sought relentlessly in countryside they did not know. There was no Hole-in-the-Wall or Robbers' Roost to escape to now.

Both Uyuni and Oruro had sizable foreign populations. Miners, fortune seekers, explorers, surveyors, visitors and tradespeople constantly drifted in and out. Both Cassidy and the Sundance Kid knew that they had to disappear into that shifting mass of foreigners, lay low for a while and then move on. With any luck, they would make it out to Santa Cruz in the eastern part of the country, and perhaps even as far as the tranquillity of the Cholila Valley and Patagonia. Here in southwestern Bolivia, given the number of soldiers, police and citizens who were busily seeking them, they were too conspicuous.

They took a twisting, narrow path beside the river. The air was heavy and oppressive. The two men turned north. The path narrowed even more as it entered a ravine. Every natural overhang seemed to scream out a warning of ambush. They continued on the path. Soon it widened again as the village of Estarca came into sight. They were forced to camp for the night, but slept fitfully. Every sound magnified the fear that a volley of shots would interrupt their rest.

Butch Cassidy and the Sundance Kid were already moving when dawn broke on November 6, 1908. Noon found them beginning the long, hard climb up toward San Vicente, a small mining village on the edge of a vast, cactus-dotted bowl high in the Cordillera Occidental.

At sundown, they rode into the town on mules. They stopped and sought shelter. The town administrator directed them to the house of Bonaficio Casasola. The owner said that they were welcome to stay in one of his patio rooms. He would get food for them and for their mounts. The weary pair gave him some pesos from the stolen payroll. As Casasola hurried off to get sardines, bread and beer, the administrator hurried straight to where a posse of soldiers was camped.

The soldiers had arrived in San Vicente that afternoon, and were part of the organized hunt for the fugitives. They tossed aside their tea, checked their rifles and followed the administrator Bellot through the darkness to Señor Casasola's house.

They stepped up to the doorway of the walled patio and paused. Only the chirping of crickets and the whisper of a light wind disturbed the quiet of the night. As the lead soldiers crossed the threshold, Cassidy appeared in the doorway of the room and ripped off a shot with his Colt. The blast fatally wounded one of the Bolivians. Butch Cassidy had murdered for the first time in his life. A barrage of gunfire drove the bandit back into the windowless room that offered no escape.

A siege ensued. The outlaws fiercely fought off all attempts by the soldiers to charge the room. The soldiers fired into the darkness sporadically while reinforcements were sent around the back to ensure that the escape routes were sealed off. A short time later, the clamor of the fight dwindled, and a tense lull ensued. Two shots were heard, but neither were aimed at the soldiers. Silence followed. Fearing a ruse, the determined soldiers stayed in their secure positions on the patio all night, despite the biting wind. The gray dawn discovered them wrapped in their ponchos, wary and alert. They forced an end to the stake-out by pushing the cowering proprietor into the room. When his eyes had accustomed themselves to the gloom, he saw Butch Cassidy sprawled on the floor, a bullet wound in his temple and another in his arm. When the soldiers joined him, they saw the Sundance Kid slumped in a sitting position, strangely embracing a large ceramic jar. He too had been wounded in the arm, but more telling was the wound in his forehead. Both men were dead. The bright career of crime had streaked to a close. The long run was over.

Or was it?

Many people feel that the hastily interred bodies were not Butch and Sundance at all. Two bodies were put in the ground of the little cemetery on the edge of San Vicente that afternoon, high in the thin air of the Andes, but some suspect that two other Americans had served for the satisfaction of the Bolivian authorities, and that Butch Cassidy and the Sundance Kid had themselves helped propagate the deception in order to escape the heat. Stories abound of their resurfacing in the American West. For years afterward, people swore that they had known and spoken with the legendary outlaws, both in South America and in the United States. The Pinkerton National Detective Agency was also thoroughly unconvinced by the story of the Bolivian police. The agents left their files open for years. Rumors of another shoot-out, this time in Uruguay, spread the rival explanation that both outlaws, together with Etta Place, did not die until 1911. Butch Cassidy's sister claimed that Butch returned to visit their father and did not die until 1937.

If, however, the first variation is the truth, one must assume that, realizing the hopelessness of the situation and running low on ammunition, the wounded Butch Cassidy fatally shot the Sundance Kid. He then put his pistol to his own head and pulled the trigger.

But whether Butch Cassidy and the Sundance Kid burnt up in the heat of their own firepower, or simply vanished from sight, is a matter that, like the fate of a shooting star, cannot certainly be determined.

BIBLIOGRAPHY & FURTHER READING

Elliott, David Stewart. *Last Raid of the Daltons: A Reliable Recital of the Battle with the Bandits at Coffeyville, Kansas, October 5, 1892.* Illust. E.A. Filleau. Coffeyville: Coffeyville Journal Print, 1892.

Etulain, Richard W., and Glenda Riley, ed. *With Badges and Bullets: Lawmen & Outlaws in the Old West.* Golden, Colorado: Fulcrum, 1999.

Garraty, John A. and Mark C. Carnes, ed. *American National Biography.* 24 vol. New York: Oxford, 1999.

Greenwood, Robert. *The California Outlaw: Tiburcio Vasquez.* Los Gatos, California: Talisman, 1960.

Hansen, Ron. *Desperadoes.* 1st ed. NewYork: Knopf, 1979.

Horan, James. *The Authentic Wild West: The Outlaws.* New York: Crown, 1976.

Kelly, Charles. *The Outlaw Trail: A History of Butch Cassidy and His Wild Bunch.* New York: Devlin-Adair, 1959.

Mather, R.E. *Hanging the Sheriff: a Biography of Henry Plummer.* University of Utah publications in the American West. Salt Lake City: University of Utah Press, 1987.

Nash, Jay Robert. *Bloodletters and Badmen: a Narrative Encyclopedia of American Criminals from the Pilgrims to the Present.* New York: M. Evans, 1973.

Nordyke, Lewis. *John Wesley Hardin, Texas Gunman.* New York: Morrow, 1957.

O'Neal, Bill. *Encyclopedia of Western Gunfighters.* Norman: University of Oklahoma Press, 1979.

Patterson, Richard. *Butch Cassidy: A Biography.* Lincoln: University of Nebraska Press, 1998.

Saint-Germain, C. de. *The Dalton Brothers and Their Astounding Career of Crime, by an Eye Witness.* Introd. Burton Rascoe. New York: Frederick Fell, 1954.

Sawyer, Eugene Taylor. *The Life and Career of Tiburcio Vasquez, the California Bandit and Murderer.* San Jose: Cottle, 1870.

Settle, William A., Jr. *Jesse James Was His Name.* Columbia: University of Missouri Press, 1966.

Utley, Robert M. *Billy the Kid: A Short and Violent Life.* Lincoln: University of Nebraska Press, 1989.